SEVEN WAYS
OF LOOKING AT
THE TRANSFIGURATION

SEVEN WAYS
OF LOOKING AT
THE TRANSFIGURATION

SARAH HINLICKY WILSON

THORNBUSH PRESS

Scripture quotations are from The ESV® Bible (The Holy Bible, English Standard Version®), copyright © 2001 by Crossway, a publishing ministry of Good News Publishers. Used by permission. All rights reserved.

Thornbush Press | www.thornbushpress.com

Book Layout © 2015 BookDesignTemplates.com
Cover Illustration and Design @eoinryanart

Seven Ways of Looking at the Transfiguration /
Sarah Hinlicky Wilson. —1st paperback ed.

ISBN 979-8-9899141-3-5

FOR THE BELOVED PEOPLE OF
TOKYO LUTHERAN CHURCH

Contents

Preface

If you follow the church year and the lectionaries that accompany it, you will celebrate the Transfiguration at least once a year—and possibly twice.

Like many festivals of the church, we don't know exactly when and where the observance of the Transfiguration began. Most likely its roots lie in the churches of Jerusalem, Palestine, and Syria, as early as the fifth century, if not earlier. By the seventh century, the Greek church in Jerusalem stipulated Scripture readings for the Transfiguration on August 6. The earliest known homily preached at a liturgical celebration of the Transfiguration dates back to this time, from a monk named Anastasius, who belonged to the monastic community of Mount Sinai.

How did August 6 become the date for the annual celebration? It obviously doesn't fall into the part of the church year that tracks the life of Christ from Christmas to Easter to Ascension. The best conjecture is that its timing is derivative of another early church celebration, the feast of the Holy Cross, which falls on September 14. Count backwards forty days from September 14 and you land on August 6. The timing makes good sense: the Transfiguration is tightly framed on either side by Jesus' first and second prophecies of his death on the cross. After he comes down from the mountain, he turns his face toward Jerusalem. The forty-day period from Transfiguration to Holy Cross thus serves as a kind of a shadow Lent in an obverse church year.

From its origins in the east, the feast of the Transfiguration gradually moved west. It first appeared in Latin liturgical manuals in the ninth century and spread out slowly over the next several centuries. The big turning point for the Transfiguration as a liturgical feast in the Western church was, not a little ironically, a military victory. Christian armies defeated the Turks at Belgrade in 1456. In thanksgiving, Pope Callixtus III formally adopted the Transfiguration into the Roman calendar. He kept its date as August 6.

It was Lutheran reformers Johannes Bugenhagen and Veit Dietrich who introduced the Transfiguration into the other half of the church year. In their revision of the church calendar, they matched the long-standing observance of the Baptism of our Lord on the first Sunday of the Epiphany season with the Transfiguration of our Lord on the last Sunday of the Epiphany season. Given the echoes between the two events in the life of Christ, this timing also makes good sense. Much like setting a fixed date for Transfiguration forty days before Holy Cross, the reassignment of Transfiguration to the last Sunday before Lent recognizes its pivotal timing in Jesus' journey toward his death. Both Baptism and Transfiguration call for the liturgical color of white, bookending an otherwise green season.

Ever since the sixteenth century, the annual observance of Transfiguration on the last Sunday of Epiphany has been the standard in Lutheran churches. In due course this timing was adopted by the Church of England, though it only came to prominence in the late nineteeenth century, and without dropping the August 6 observance. Nowadays, any Protestant church following the Revised Common Lectionary will, at least by default, observe the Transfiguration annually on the last Sunday of Epiphany. The Roman Catholic Church maintains the fixed date in August but also stipulates a Gospel reading about the Transfiguration on the second Sunday in Lent, with similar intent to the Reformation churches. Transfiguration continues to be observed on August 6 only by the Orthodox churches.[1]

Though late to start and slow to spread, the liturgical celebration of the Transfiguration testifies to its enormous importance in both the life of Christ and the interpretation of his redeeming work in time and eternity.

And yet, when was the last time you heard anyone, preacher or otherwise, speak of its enormous importance?

There is no end of reflection on the incarnation at Christmas, the strange victory of the cross on Good Friday, or the greater victory of triumph over sin and death on Easter. Even Pentecost has made a comeback in the last century, thanks to the Christians who named themselves for the outpouring of the Holy Spirit. But what have you got for Transfiguration?

I felt this aporia when I returned to parish ministry after a long spell in ecumenical and scholarly work. I enjoyed preaching on Transfiguration the first time. In my second year I stretched to find something to say. In the third, I resorted to the Greek and happily discovered the word "exodus" in Luke's account. But by the fourth year, I had to conclude: I have nothing left to say on the Transfiguration.

And then I thought: that can't possibly be right. I cannot have plumbed all of the Transfiguration's depths in just three sermons. *Surely* there is more going on here than I've realized so far.

So I started digging. It didn't take very long to discover yes, there is a *lot* more going on here than I realized. All I had to do was tug on one slender thread within the Transfiguration story to find that it was connected to an intricate, gorgeous web stretching across the whole of Scripture. Keep tugging, keep finding. I settled on seven ways of looking at the Transfiguration, but I promise you that even the hundred and twenty pages of this book do not exhaust the possibilities!

I hope, though, that these seven ways of looking at the Transfiguration will be more than enough to keep you eagerly returning to this story year after year, whether you are a faithful follower of Christ treasuring all these things in your heart or a preacher proclaiming the Gospel for the upbuilding of your congregation.

A few notes about what follows.

To map out the intricate interconnections across the Scriptures, I've tracked words through both Testaments. Greek words in quotations are denoted in English transliteration in the exact form they take in the New Testament, including diacritical marks. Greek words referred to outside of direct quotations appear in their dictionary form.

Hebrew words are denoted in simplified English transliteration, without diacritical marks (which are considerably more extensive than in Greek if you are trying to be strictly accurate). Moreover, Hebrew words appear in their basic dictionary form, rather than their exact appearance in the Old Testament, because there is so much more variation as they are conjugated, declined, prefixed, or suffixed that they will be less obviously the same words to English-language readers unfamiliar with Hebrew.

You will see in these pages Greek words from the Old Testament, too. That is not as self-contradictory as it sounds. Greek was already the universal language across the Mediterranean centuries before Jesus' time. Jews in Palestine as well as in the diaspora knew Greek and used it extensively. In the third century before Christ they made translations of their originally Hebrew Scriptures into Greek, for their own use as well as for the edification of interested Gentiles. The New Testament authors were well acquainted with these translations and often used them—though sometimes they made their own translations or used local variations. The standard ancient Greek version of the Old Testament is called, in English, the Septuagint, which derives from Latin for "seventy," referring to the seventy (actually seventy-two) Jewish elders believed to have translated the Torah identically all at the same time. For this reason it is sometimes abbreviated as LXX, which are the Roman numerals for seventy.

The reason to refer to the Septuagint when undertaking a canonical interpretation of a Gospel story, as I'm doing here, is this. Since the Greek-speaking and -writing authors of the New Testament knew the LXX, they would often intentionally select its choice of Greek words when they wanted to echo and allude to the same Old Testament passages. That gives us strong clues toward their theological intentions. When Greek words from the Septuagint are noted in this book, they appear in the exact form they take in the text, diacritical marks and all.

Certain events in Jesus' life are designated with a capital letter to distinguish them from what could, in principle, be experienced by someone else: thus the Baptism, Transfiguration, Passion, Crucifixion, Resurrection, and Ascension of Jesus. Many people have gotten baptized, but the Baptism with a capital B refers to Jesus alone. I also follow the convention of small caps for "LORD" or "Lord GOD" when it indicates the unpronounced holy name hiding in the background, but only in direct biblical quotations from Old Testament Hebrew.

The Transfiguration event is recorded in the Gospels of Mark, Matthew, Luke, and in the Second Epistle of Peter. I list them in this order because I assume, along with the vast majority of biblical scholars, that Mark's was the first Gospel to be written down, and was known to both Matthew and Luke, who used it as the basis of their own Gospels, which is why the three of them together are called the "Synoptic" Gospels—they see together (*syn*) with one eye (*optic*). The relatively unknown and unloved Second Epistle of Peter is probably one of the latest-written books of the New Testament, but it also includes an account of the Transfiguration. I have made my own translations of these four biblical accounts of the Transfiguration, which are interspersed between the chapters that follow. When I quote from these specific sections, I am using my own translations. Other quotations from the Bible are taken from the English Standard Version, unless otherwise noted.

MARK 9:1–10

1 And he was saying to them:
Amen I say to you all
that there are certain ones of those standing here,
the same ones will no way, no how taste death
until they should have seen
the kingdom of God
having come in power.

2 And after six days
Jesus takes along
Peter and James and John,
and he bears them up
to a high mountain
by themselves alone.

And he was transfigured
in front of them,

3 and his clothes became
extremely gleaming white
in such a way
a bleacher upon the earth
could not whiten them.

4 And there appeared to them Elijah,
with Moses,
and they were talking together with Jesus.

5 And Peter
speaking up
said to Jesus,

Rabbi,
it is good for us to be here,
and let us make three tabernacles,
one for you and

one for Moses and
one for Elijah.

6 For he did not know
how to speak up,
for they'd come to be frightened out of their wits.

7 And a cloud
came to be overshadowing them,
and a voice came to be from the cloud:

This is my Son,
the beloved;
listen to him.

8 And all at once
looking around
they no longer saw anybody
but Jesus alone
with them.

9 And them descending
from the mountain
he charged them
that they describe
what they saw
to not one single person,

until when
the Son of Man
should rise from the dead.

10 And they held back the word to themselves,
disputing what it is,
to rise from the dead.

METAMORPHOSIS : JESUS

If you want to meet God, then go either to a desert or to a mountain.

John went to the desert, no less deserted for the river in its midst, to contemplate the pathways of God and preach repentance in hope of the forgiveness of sins. He fed on locusts and wild honey and attracted sinners and hypocrites for company.

Jesus also went to the desert, though one without a river, having only stones for food and the devil for company. Then he returned to the towns and cities and the byways in between them, preaching repentance, forgiveness—and more besides.

Having already done the desert, halfway through his sojourn, "after six days Jesus takes along Peter and James and John, and he bears them up to a high mountain by themselves alone" (Mark 9:2).

The vagueness of the mountain's name and location has long frustrated piety. Mark and Matthew say only "a high mountain." Luke refers to "*the* mountain," as if you should know the antecedent already. The curious dark-horse witness of Second Peter calls it "the holy mountain." But that begs more questions than it answers. It is holy because of what happened to Jesus there? Or was it holy to begin with?

You might be tempted think the designation "holy" makes Mount Sinai the obvious choice. After all, it's the one mountain where the Lord God did actually appear in flashing light and clouds and glory.

But in the Scriptures of Israel, "the holy mountain" is *never* Mount Sinai. "The holy mountain" is always and only Mount Zion in Jerusalem on which the temple stands—or possibly an eschatological extension thereof. Thus Psalms 48 and 99, three major prophets (Isaiah, Ezekiel, and Daniel), and four minor prophets (Joel, Obadiah, Zephaniah, and Zechariah).

Yet Mount Zion in Jerusalem cannot possibly be where Jesus took his inner circle, among other reasons because it is impossible to be *alone* there! Anyway, in Synoptic logic, it is much too soon for Jesus to be anywhere near Jerusalem. The mountaintop moment marks his turn south *toward* Jerusalem, temple, and the cross. So we must look elsewhere for our mountain.

Up to this point, in Mark's telling, Jesus has been in the neighborhood of the Sea of Galilee, close to his adult hometown of Capernaum, crossing the sea by boat and healing a blind man in Bethsaida. From there he pushes on to the northernmost point of his earthly life, the villages around Caesarea Philippi.

For sheer proximity to the area, the best mountainous candidate is Mount Hermon. It is scripturally resonant, too, a boundary marker of the promised land and evocative in its snow-capped majesty. Psalm 133 compares the goodness and pleasantness of brothers dwelling in unity to "the dew of Hermon, which falls on the mountains of Zion!" Maybe in this way Mount Hermon borrows some of Mount Zion's distinctive holiness.

However, in the early 200s, church father Origen awarded the distinction to Mount Tabor, and it has been known as the mountain of the Transfiguration ever since. Churches have stood on Mount Tabor since at least the fourth century; the bishop of Tabor attended the Fifth Ecumenical Council in Constantinople in 553.

In favor of Origen's choice, Mount Tabor lies close to Nazareth on the way back south from Caesarea Philippi, a place you might well pass if you were planning to carry on all the way to Jerusalem. You'd easily reach it "after six days" of leisurely hiking. Tabor, like Hermon, serves as a boundary marker for the land of Israel. It is the site of battle chosen by Deborah, prophetess and judge, to confront the armies of Sisera.

The truth is, we don't know for sure which mountain it was. What we do know for sure is that a holy thing happened there, enough to render any remote, second-rate, or forgotten mountain luminous with holiness.

They reach the top, and the thing happens. "He was transfigured in front of them."

The word itself has become luminous. In our Latin-derived

English, we only use it of Jesus, and only in this instance. We even bestow upon the noun the distinction of a definite article and a capital letter: *the* Transfiguration.

But in the simplest sense of the Greek that lies behind it, *metemorphōthē*, it's an ordinary word. *Meta*: beyond. *Morphḗ*: form or figure. Combined, placed in the past tense and the passive voice, all it means is "changed."

All it means? As if it were obvious what change is! How can something be something else? Is it still itself? Is there continuity of identity, or rupture? Does the change reveal what was always there but hidden, or does it create something entirely new? If one form dissolves and another appears, does the reality behind the form perdure, or vanish? What is the relationship between being and becoming?

A simple word, yet in its wake "change" drags along one of the most ancient, most fundamental, least understood, least resolved questions in the entire history of human thought.

The impossible, impenetrable simplicity of the problem is revealed by the chief English use of the noun taken right from the Greek, "metamorphosis," to describe how a caterpillar becomes a butterfly. The transitional state is the chrysalis. You would assume that the caterpillar inside the chrysalis does something straightforward and sensible, like sprouting wings from its existing body. That is, after all, what it looks like on the other side: a caterpillar with wings.

But in fact, once sealed inside its living tomb, the biological entity that is the caterpillar dissolves. It actually digests itself! It is formless and void, a molecular chaos, or to put it in the vernacular, goo. The tiniest fraction of cells survives the process, reassembling the goo into a butterfly. And so the resulting creature is and isn't itself; it remains the same and becomes something different; its lifespan is both continuous and radically severed.

So to assert that Jesus was "changed," "metamorphosed," "transfigured" in front of them says entirely too little. Or entirely too much! Luke deletes the word altogether, likely because, as an elegant rhetorician in the Greek language, he suspected it would connote metamorphoses of the pagan type: Zeus metamorphosing into a golden shower in order to violate the unsuspecting Danaë, for instance.[2] Whatever the change in Jesus signifies, it doesn't signify *that*.

In any case, all three Evangelists immediately need to furnish further details.

Mark swiftly shifts the focus. *Jesus* was transfigured, he writes, yet the visible result was only that "his clothes became extremely gleaming white in such a way a bleacher upon the earth could not whiten them" (9:3). That word "gleaming," *stílbonta*, is what's called a hapax legomenon, a one-off in New Testament vocabulary—though Homer used it in the Iliad. "Shining," "glittering," or "radiant" could all work, too. The point is the brilliance, the degree ("extremely"), and the uniqueness in kind.

But in case you don't quite grasp how remarkable this is—that the metamorphosis is not of this earth—Mark adds a further down-home detail. Jesus' clothing is white in a way that exceeds the technical skill of laundry specialists. The old-fashioned English term "fuller" is often used in translations. The task of "fulling" stands in for the whole range of tasks involved in preparing wool for spinning, including cleaning it and fluffing it up—"fulling" it. The Greek term is *gnapheùs* (another New Testament hapax legomenon), meaning the person who cards the wool with brushes to prepare it for spinning. The wool needs to be cleaned before carding, with something fast and noxious like lye or slow and pleasant like the sun. The cleaning process bleaches, hence the whiteness. But only up to a point.

What's going on in Jesus' Transfiguration isn't a matter of materials science. Washing, bleaching, and purifying all imply their opposite: that up till now, the garment or person in question was dirty. Hence David prays in Psalm 51:7, "Purge me with hyssop, and I shall be clean; wash me, and I shall be whiter than snow." The Lord accuses through Jeremiah, "Though you wash yourself with lye and use much soap, the stain of your guilt is still before me" (2:22), and later pleads through the same prophet, "O Jerusalem, wash your heart from evil, that you may be saved" (4:14). Daniel foresees a time when "some of the wise shall stumble, so that they may be refined, purified, and made white" (11:35, cf. 12:10). Malachi warns that the day of the Lord is not what you think it is: "But who can endure the day of his coming, and who can stand when he appears? For he is like a refiner's fire and like fullers' soap" (3:2).

If Jesus' garments were only just as white as what a fuller or *gnapheùs* could manage, then he would be a purified man ready for the day of the Lord. But *only* that. Only a sinner in need of purification who just so happens to have undergone it. Mark wants you to understand we are not talking about *that* kind of whiter-than-snow garment. The Transfiguration that comes upon Jesus is something altogether different.

Matthew drops the fuller analogy, Luke does, too, and both expand Mark's spartan description, each in his own direction.

Echoing Mark, Matthew says Jesus "was transfigured in front of them," but he looks first to Jesus' face. It shone, *élampsen*, whence English "lamp," like the sun.

Matthew likes shining as a metaphor. In the Sermon on the Mount, Jesus had already taught, "Nor do people light a lamp and put it under a basket, but on a stand, and it gives light [*lámpei*] to all in the house. In the same way, let your light shine [*lampsátō*] before others, so that they may see your good works and give glory to your Father who is in heaven" (5:15–16). Do so and you will count among the righteous, who "will shine out [*eklámpsousin*] like the sun in the kingdom of their Father" (13:43, alluding to Daniel 12:3).

But where are the righteous to be found? Only Jesus shines like the sun, and only here on the mountaintop. When he is crucified, the sun itself will go out. "Now from the sixth hour there was darkness over all the land until the ninth hour" (27:45). It is no accident that news of the risen Jesus comes "toward the dawn" (28:1).

Still. The sun is an ambivalent choice of image, probably avoided with reason by both Mark and Luke. The cloud—as we will see in a later chapter—is much preferred as the meteorological vehicle of the Lord's Presence. The sun, by contrast, is regularly put in its place as an obedient creation serving the Lord's good pleasure, perhaps in memory of the sun-worship practiced by the Egyptians or in competition with the sun-worship practiced by the Canaanites, Babylonians, and Persians. Deuteronomy warns against lifting your eyes to heaven and bowing down before "the sun and the moon and the stars" (4:19), "which I have forbidden" (17:3), a danger that becomes a reality in the times of the kings (II Kings 23:5, 11; Jeremiah 8:1–2).

Ezekiel has a potent vision of the rivalry. He is carried away in the Spirit by "a form that had the appearance of a man. Below what appeared to be his waist was fire, and above his waist was something like the appearance of brightness, like gleaming metal" (8:2). In the inner court of the house of the Lord, between the porch and the altar, the prophet witnesses "about twenty-five men, with their backs to the temple of the LORD, and their faces toward the east, worshiping the sun toward the east" (8:16). It's the culminating abomination of many abominations in the temple. The Lord promises to have no pity on them.

In fact, the only unambiguous, unqualified association of the God of Israel with the sun appears in one verse of one Psalm: "For the LORD God is a sun and shield" (Psalm 84:11).

The next-best usage is a generous simile for an excellent ruler like David. As the king himself says in his last words, "When one rules justly over men, ruling in the fear of God, he dawns on them like the morning light, like the sun shining forth on a cloudless morning" (II Samuel 23:3–4).

If Matthew wished only to emphasize Jesus standing in the house and lineage of David as its rightful heir, then the simile stands. But worthy as this is, it's altogether inadequate for the Evangelist's christological goals.

More likely Matthew is asserting the accomplished victory of the Lord over his rival the sun, such as the prophet Isaiah foresaw and the Book of Revelation repeats: "The sun shall be no more your light by day, nor for brightness shall the moon give you light; but the LORD will be your everlasting light, and your God will be your glory. Your sun shall no more go down, nor your moon withdraw itself; for the LORD will be your everlasting light, and your days of mourning shall be ended" (Isaiah 60:19–20, cf. Revelation 21:22–25, 22:4–5).

For all that, the contrast might not be so much Jesus-versus-the-sun as Jesus-versus-the-disciples. On the mountaintop, the face of

Jesus radiates light. On the same mountaintop, the disciples "fell on their faces and were exceedingly frightened" (Matthew 17:6).

Luke agrees with Matthew that more is happening with Jesus than his exceptional attire. But he is wary, on several levels, of how his Synoptic brothers have reported the story.

So first of all, having as he does a particular interest in Jesus' prayer life, Luke sets the whole Transfiguration in the context of prayer.[3] While Mark and Matthew's versions could be construed as a casual walk or a vigorous hike, Luke makes it one of many instances of Jesus going away in private to pray (cf. 9:18, 11:1, 22:41). Jesus had already made a habit of withdrawing to the desert (5:16) and the mountain (6:12) to pray: the usual places you go to meet God. That the Transfiguration should come upon him on the latter, not in the former, sets Jesus apart from John—another particular interest of Luke's.[4]

And so, "he ascended the mountain to pray. And in his praying the appearance of his face came to be different" (9:28–29). As noted above, Luke drops the word "metamorphosed." But he concedes that the face became "different" (*heteron*). How different and in what way, Luke refrains from clarifying. Actually, he puts in a further buffer to clarity by saying that the "appearance" (*eîdos*) of Jesus' face is what became different. This Greek word indicates the visible manifestation of something—it derives from the verb "to see"—but can mean form or shape, much the same as the *morphḗ* in metamorphosis.

Luke's apparent hedging points to the age-old problem of relating a transcendent vision accurately. The first chapter of Ezekiel, for example, reads like a chain of barriers to comprehension, while in fact being the prophet's only way of helping you even begin to comprehend. Repeatedly he deploys words and phrases like "as it were," "as for the likeness," and "like the appearance."

And that's just for creatures. When it comes to God, Ezekiel practically stutters in his effort to depict what exceeds the senses. "There was the likeness of a throne, in appearance like sapphire; and seated above the likeness of a throne was a likeness with a human appearance... And downward from what had the appearance of his waist I saw as it were the appearance of fire... Such was the appearance of the likeness of the glory of the LORD" (1:26–28). Luke is the only one of the Evangelists to use the word "glory" in the Transfiguration. He has learned from Ezekiel the impossibility of describing glory—and the necessity of trying to do so anyway.

As it turns out, at the Transfiguration Jesus' face becomes "different" in more ways than one. Very soon afterwards, he will "set his face to go to Jerusalem" (Luke 9:51). And he's told us twice already what's going to happen to him when he gets there.

Matthew and Luke both return to Jesus' clothing and its exceptional whiteness. The first says "his clothes came to be white like light" (17:2), the second that they were "lightning-white" (9:29). Either way, they concur with Mark: this kind of whiteness does not lie within the realm of earthly possibilities.

Here we are back on safer ground. White garments have a long symbolic reach, backwards into Israel and forwards into the eschaton.

Luke can, in fact, reach right back into that first chapter of Ezekiel to borrow the Septuagint's term: *exastráptōn*, dazzling or flashing like lightning. "As I looked, a stormy wind came out of the north: a great cloud with brightness [*exastrápton*] around it and fire flashing forth continually and in the middle of the fire something like gleaming amber... Their legs were straight, and the soles of their feet were like the sole of a calf's foot, and they sparkled like burnished [*exastráptōn*] bronze" (Ezekiel 1:4, 7).[5] In Ezekiel, the cloud is what dazzles like lightning, but in the Transfiguration, Jesus' garments are what dazzle. That's Luke's subtle way of stacking up and overlapping the respective identities of the Lord God and his beloved Son.

Even more important than Ezekiel's is the role the prophet Daniel plays in the background of the Transfiguration—and, indeed, in much of the Gospels' depiction of Jesus. As this prophetic book turns from fiery furnaces and lions' dens to wild and disturbing visions, two figures take center stage.

First, "as I looked, thrones were placed, and the Ancient of Days took his seat; his clothing was white as snow, and the hair of his head like pure wool; his throne was fiery flames; its wheels were burning fire. A stream of fire issued and came out from before him" (7:9–10). White and light characterize this figure.

Then comes the second. "And behold, with the clouds of heaven there came one like a son of man, and he came to the Ancient of Days and was presented before him. And to him was given dominion and glory and a kingdom, that all peoples, nations, and languages should serve him; his dominion is an everlasting dominion, which shall not pass away, and his kingdom one that shall not be destroyed" (7:13–14). The association with both the clouds and the Ancient of Days is evocative, but this second figure's identity remains underdetermined, until chapter 10.

There, after an extended period of fasting, Daniel beholds "a man clothed in linen, with a belt of fine gold from Uphaz around his waist. His body was like beryl, his face like the appearance of lightning [astrapês], his eyes like flaming torches, his arms and legs like the gleam of burnished [stílbontos] bronze, and the sound of his words like the sound of a multitude" (5–6). As in Ezekiel's report, Daniel has to buffer his observations with qualifications: "one in the likeness of the children of man" or "one having the appearance of a man" (16, 18).

Note that there is a certain range permissible here. The exact appearance of the remarkable figure isn't nailed down, in part because it can't be. What in any case could be meant by a "face like the appearance of lightning"? The Evangelists draw on a general set of qualities circling around the "son of man": his whiteness, lightness, and brightness.

Ay, there's the rub. Radiant white light is *so* evocative that it can't be contained just to a divine figure. It bounces around and shines everywhere.

So in a much later apocalyptic book, greatly inspired by both Ezekiel and Daniel, whiteness is distributed prodigally. In Revelation there are white hairs (1:14), white stones (2:17), white horses (6:2, 19:11), white clouds (14:14), and a white throne (20:11). Above all, white garments (3:4–5, 3:18, 4:4, 6:11, 7:9, 7:13–14, 19:14). Yet it is not the crucified and risen Lord Jesus who is arrayed in white, but those he has gathered and preserved for himself, from martyrs to elders.

The only unmistakable application of this set of images to Jesus appears in the first chapter of Revelation. John of Patmos sees "one like a son of man, clothed with a long robe and with a golden sash around his chest. The hairs of his head were white, like white wool, like snow. His eyes were like a flame of fire, his feet were like burnished bronze, refined in a furnace, and his voice was like the roar of many waters. In his right hand he held seven stars, from his mouth came a sharp two-edged sword, and his face was like the sun shining in full strength" (1:13–16). To apply the term that Revelation does not, this Jesus is *transfigured*.

And this in turn points us toward a mystery that will require the rest of the book to solve.

In the accounts of his Resurrection, Jesus is absolutely, certainly, definitely *not* the figure robed in white or dazzling like lightning. At precisely the moment you'd *most* expect him to be set apart by his appearance, he isn't. The risen Jesus is in fact so unremarkable that Mary Magdalene doesn't recognize him at first, nor his companions on the road to Emmaus, nor his disciples on the boat squinting at the seashore.

More strangely still, the whiteness, lightness, and brightness are transferred to others—unnamed messengers at best. Mark reports how the women, upon entering the tomb, "saw a young man sitting on the right side, dressed in a white robe, and they were alarmed" (16:5). His robe is not whiter than a bleacher could manage, but distinctly white all the same.

Matthew employs images he didn't use for the Transfiguration but that draw on the same prophetic sources: "And behold, there was a great earthquake, for an angel of the Lord descended from heaven and came and rolled back the stone and sat on it. His appearance was like lightning [*astrapè*], and his clothing white as snow" (Matthew 28:2–3). The angel, *not* Jesus.

Luke puts a similar figure at the Resurrection—"While they were perplexed about this, behold, two men stood by them in dazzling [*astraptoúsē*] apparel" (24:4)—and also at the Ascension—"And while they were gazing into heaven as he went, behold, two men stood by them in white robes" (Acts 1:10).

The unnamed messengers bear some resemblance to the transfigured Jesus, but not at all to the risen Jesus.

More to the point, the *transfigured* Jesus bears almost no resemblance to the *risen* Jesus!

The Evangelists do not intend you to doubt that the Jesus of the Transfiguration and the Jesus of the Resurrection are the same Jesus. Most certainly, he is one and the same Jesus.

What they want you to grasp, rather, is that the Transfiguration and the Resurrection are telling you two distinct things about the same Jesus. They are not to be interchanged or collapsed. To lose either is to lose something crucial about Jesus.

So if it's not a preview of the Resurrection, then what *is* the Transfiguration?

What can it mean for one and the same Jesus, eternal and everlasting, to *change*?

Eschaton : Elijah

As if the Transfiguration of Jesus' clothing to lightning-linen weren't astounding enough, suddenly two of the all-stars of Israel's history appear for a tête-à-tête with him.

The commonplace interpretation is that these two represent "the Law and the Prophets," with Moses standing in for the first and Elijah for the second.

That's handy, but it's probably wrong.

For one thing, Moses may have been the transmitter of the Law from the Lord God to the people of Israel, but he was remembered just as much as a prophet. If anything, as the prophet *par excellence*. Moses reports how the Lord said to him, "I will raise up for them a prophet like you from among their brothers" (Deuteronomy 18:18, quoted by Peter in Acts 3:22), and the same book closes with the sentiment, "there has not arisen a prophet since in Israel like Moses, whom the LORD knew face to face" (34:10).

For another thing, Elijah is only modestly acclaimed as prophet in his own live-action stories (such as in I Kings 18:22, 18:36, 19:16, and II Chronicles 21:12). If anything, accounts of Elijah allude rather to cohorts of other prophets, variously in service to the Lord or to Baal. The terms "man of God," "servant of God," and "troubler of Israel" are more often applied to Elijah, by contrast to the steady reference to, say, Samuel or Nathan as prophets. Not to mention the fact that there is no book of Elijah among the prophetic writings.

No, some other logic selects Moses and Elijah from all the candidates in Israel's history to confer with Jesus on the mountaintop.[6]

A first reason for the appearance of Moses and Elijah is that they are mountaintop men.

Although the mountain of Transfiguration is not Mount Sinai, and Mount Sinai is not "the holy mountain," both Moses and Elijah meet with God on Mount Sinai (the preferred name in Exodus), also known as Mount Horeb (the preferred name in Deuteronomy). More than that, *only* Moses and Elijah ascend Sinai/Horeb for direct conversation with God. No other person in the Scriptures does the same.

Moses spends forty days and forty nights on Sinai. Elijah takes forty days to reach Horeb.

Both Moses and Elijah long to behold God in all his glory. Neither gets exactly what he hoped for, in converse ways. Moses does see God's glory but not his face, "for man shall not see me and live" (Exodus 33:20). Elijah, by contrast, feels the force of a strong wind, an earthquake, and a fire, yet what turns out to be God's Presence is a still small voice (I Kings 19:12).

So what dazzles the eyes of the disciples at the Transfiguration is actually God cloaked in manageable majesty for Moses and Elijah. At last they get to see what they always wanted to see: the face of God in the gloriously transfigured Jesus. Who himself would remark, "Many prophets and righteous people longed to see what you see, and did not see it, and to hear what you hear, and did not hear it" (Matthew 13:17).

Another reason for the pairing of Moses and Elijah is their mysterious exit from this mortal life.

Moses was denied entrance to the promised land. His last sight from the heights of Mount Nebo was of the plains stretching out to the sea. "Moses the servant of the LORD died there in the land of Moab, according to the word of the LORD, and he buried him in the valley in the land of Moab opposite Beth-peor; but no one knows the place of his burial to this day" (Deuteronomy 34:5–6). For being such a famous figure, Moses ended up with no memorial shrine. The Lord buried him and him alone directly, in a grave no living person ever saw or found.

Elijah, for his part, occupies no earthly grave at all. As he spoke with his successor Elisha, "behold, chariots of fire and horses of fire separated the two of them. And Elijah went up by a whirlwind into heaven" (II Kings 2:11).

Jesus, too, would go on to die according to the word of the Lord, and in a sense even be buried by the Lord's explicit authorization.

On the other side of his death, he too would depart in non-standard fashion by ascending into heaven. Jesus encompasses all manners and modes of leaving earthly life.

A sixth-century deacon named Pantoleon explains the pairing of Elijah and Moses this way: "Because Elijah was numbered with the living, but Moses is dead, and for that reason, through the presence of both, [Jesus] revealed himself to them as Lord of the living and the dead, clearly teaching those who were present, by these signs, that he himself has authority over life and death."[7] Whatever the nature of their existence, Elijah and Moses are most certainly not ghosts or wraiths of the underworld. Living, dead, either way: the Lord is their Lord, and he can bring them to the mountaintop.

And so these two mysteriously departed personages foreshadow what Paul would write much later: "For to this end Christ died and lived again, that he might be Lord both of the dead and of the living" (Romans 14:9).

A third reason for electing Moses and Elijah among all the luminaries of Israel is that both anointed successors rich in the Spirit of God.

The first mention of Moses's successor Joshua, in Exodus 17, sends him to battle against the Amalekites, while Moses himself ascends to the top of an unnamed hill along with two companions, Aaron and Hur. Moses's uplifted hands, supported by his left flank and his right flank, guarantee Joshua's victory.

Joshua may also have accompanied Moses "up into the mountain of God" (Exodus 24:13). It's not quite clear whether he went all the way up or not, but if he did, it would make Joshua the only one of the wilderness generation besides Moses to do so. In any case, Joshua counts among the select group of those who climb the heights halfway up for congress with the Lord.

More significantly still, when Moses's final hours are drawing near, he asks God to appoint a leader in his place, "that the congregation of the LORD may not be as sheep that have no shepherd" (Numbers 27:17, cf. Mark 6:34). The Lord elects "Joshua the son of Nun, a man in whom is the Spirit" (27:18).

In another account of Joshua's commissioning, we are told that "Joshua the son of Nun was full of the spirit of wisdom, for Moses had laid his hands on him" (Deuteronomy 34:9). This Joshua would go on to perform enough mighty deeds to get an entire book named after him. Subduing Canaanites is pretty impressive, but the most resonant of Joshua's deeds was stopping the flow of the Jordan to allow the tribes to cross with the ark of the covenant, recalling Moses's parting of the Red Sea.

Above all, Joshua gets a Savior named after him. Jesus is the English adaptation of Iēsoûs, which is the Greek adaptation of Yehoshua, which is the Hebrew source for the English Joshua.

Elijah, for his part, reaches the end of his rope on Mount Horeb. The still small voice hears out his bitter complaint about being left all alone and under threat of death, and in turn comforts him with the promise of a companion: "Elisha the son of Shaphat of Abel-meholah you shall anoint to be prophet in your place" (I Kings 19:16).

Other than boiling a yoke of oxen, Elisha does nothing remarkable until the time comes for Elijah's departure. Then he proves to be as stubbornly faithful as Ruth was to Naomi. "As the LORD lives, and as you yourself live, I will not leave you" (II Kings 2:2, 4, 6). Elisha follows doggedly as Elijah smacks the Jordan to make it part for them to pass, like Moses and Joshua did before him.

In the prophets' final moments together, Elisha asks, "Please let there be a double portion of your spirit on me" (2:9). Elijah avers that this is a hard thing, but if Elisha sees for himself Elijah's unusual departure, he'll know he's gotten the double-Spirit-portion.

Elisha does see it. He tests the Spirit by taking up Elijah's cloak and smacking the Jordan while crying out, "Where is the LORD, the God of Elijah?" Near at hand, evidently. For the fourth and final time, the waters part for a servant of God.

All this is what Moses and Elijah have in common: mountains, mysterious deaths, Spirited successors. Now it is time to consider what sets them apart, why each individually needs to be present at the Transfiguration of the Lord.

We'll begin with Elijah, because Mark does.

And that, already, is strange.

As a matter of course, Moses should get pride of place. He was called by God from the burning bush; confronted Pharaoh; led the children of Israel through the Red Sea; spoke to God face to face; transmitted the law; became the prophet of prophets until Christ himself.

If nothing else, Moses precedes Elijah *chronologically*! It just makes more sense to put him first. Matthew and Luke thought so; they flip Mark's order.

But it's not like Mark didn't know perfectly well that Moses should come first. If he put Elijah first instead, he had good reason for doing so.

It turns out that a lot hinges on Elijah. The true identity of Elijah forms a major subplot in the Gospel of Mark; one that continues, in transfigured fashion, as the subplot about whose baptism confers God's Spirit in the double volume of Luke-Acts.[8]

The Transfiguration account is flanked on either side by closely related reports. On the near end, there's Peter's confession that Jesus is the Christ and Jesus' first prophecy of his own death and Resurrection (8:27–33). On the far end, there's Jesus' warning to say nothing of what they had seen until after his Resurrection and the disciples' bafflement about "what it is, to rise from the dead" (9:10).

Both times, Elijah almost steals the spotlight from Jesus.

"Who do people say that I am?" Jesus asks his disciples en route to Caesarea Philippi. They answer, "John the Baptist; and others say, Elijah; and others, one of the prophets" (8:27–28).

It's not the first time we've heard this answer. As Jesus' fame grew, he was mistaken for and conflated with John the Baptist, a prospect deeply alarming to Herod, who oversaw that inconvenient gadfly's beheading. Jesus was also taken for "a prophet, like one of the prophets of old," or, of course, "Elijah" (Mark 6:14–16).

After the Transfiguration, Jesus for a second time warns Peter, James, and John about his imminent death and its surprising sequel. They are too unnerved to press him on it. So they punt. "Why do the scribes say that first Elijah must come?" (9:11). Meaning, presumably, that Elijah is supposed to return before anyone rises from the dead.

Jesus confirms that "Elijah does come first to restore all things" (9:12). Or—possibly—he puts it back to them as a rhetorical question: "*Does* Elijah come first to restore all things?" Because what follows is half an affirmation and half a disputation. Yes, Jesus agrees, Elijah comes first, indeed "Elijah *has* come." But, plain to see, not all things have been restored! So where does the failure lie: with Elijah or Elijah-presumptive, or with the scribal interpretation of Elijah's coming?

Jesus sends his disciples back to the Scriptures. Consider afresh how it is written of the Son of Man that he should suffer many things and be despised. And if the Son of Man, so also Elijah. The disciples won't be able to catch hold of a fiery chariot to transport them out of suffering. And for that matter, this time around, neither will Elijah. For "Elijah has come, and they did to him whatever they pleased, as it is written of him" (9:13).

In other words, the Scriptures teach that what Elijah brings is *not* restoration, but a foretaste of suffering.

So why *did* the scribes think that an eschatological Elijah would come and restore all things?

The Gospel of Mark opens with a quote attributed to Isaiah, but it's actually a pastiche of Malachi and Isaiah. The Malachi part reads, "Behold, I send my messenger before your face, who will prepare your way" (Mark 1:2). In Malachi's prophecy, the very next arrival after the messenger is the Lord himself, who "will suddenly come to his temple," but the focus immediately shifts back to the messenger again: "The messenger of the covenant in whom you delight, behold, he is coming, says the LORD of hosts." All this just in Malachi 3:1.

Delight runs its course quickly. In the very next verse, the prophet asks, "But who can endure the day of his coming, and who can stand when he appears? For he is like a refiner's fire and like fullers' soap"— like a launderer who washes and scrubs and bleaches to restore soiled clothing to its pristine state! This messenger will purify the sons of Levi, Judah, and Jerusalem, until they are pleasing to the Lord again. Then, says the Lord, "I will draw near to you for judgment" (3:2–5).

So far we have a messenger. Moreover, a messenger who will set things right—restore the lost and erring children of Israel to their pure state in anticipation of the Lord's coming. But we don't yet have Elijah.

Flip the page, though, to Malachi 4, and you get not just Elijah but Moses along with him, making this the fourth reason for their paired appearance on the mount of Transfiguration. The Lord of hosts has repeated his warning that "the day is coming," one of blazing judgment upon evildoers but vindication of those who fear his name. In conclusion, the Lord declares: "Remember the law of my servant Moses, the statutes and rules that I commanded him at Horeb for all Israel. Behold, I will send you Elijah the prophet before the great and awesome day of the LORD comes. And he will turn the hearts of fathers to their children and the hearts of children to their fathers, lest I come and strike the land with a decree of utter destruction" (4:4–6).

With that, the prophecy of Malachi draws to a close. Christians would later arrange the Scriptures of Israel so that this would be the last word of the Old Testament. Turn the page of a Christian Bible and the next thing you will find is the genealogy of Jesus in Matthew 1.

And yet.

If a chosen messenger of the Lord is coming, a "messenger of the covenant in whom you delight," who will purify like a launderer's soap and make the children of Israel pleasing to the Lord again, someone of the stature of Moses and Elijah—wouldn't it make the most sense to associate this figure with *Jesus*?

Isn't that exactly what the Malachi-to-Matthew arrangement suggests: *Jesus* as new-Elijah, not John? Mark starts his Gospel with our accustomed candidate for new-Elijah, namely John the Baptist, but Matthew heading up the New Testament doesn't get around to John until chapter 3. The arrangers of the canon evidently weren't too worried about any potential confusion, though. By their time the identity of new-Elijah, and the relationship of John to Jesus, had been worked out, settled, and put to rest.

But we can detect inside the Gospels that a struggle took place. It is self-evident to us *now* that John-as-new-Elijah was the forerunner of Jesus. But it must not have been so self-evident at the time.

So let's back up and start again with Mark. The first mention of Elijah does *not* occur in conjunction with John's first appearance or Jesus' Baptism—which you might expect following a quotation, even a misattributed one, from Malachi. No, Elijah isn't even mentioned until John the Baptist is dead!

Herod, a real "troubler of Israel," has granted his stepdaughter Salome's request for a certain someone's head on a platter, and apparently not without regret—though not enough regret for him to lose face in front of his party guests. Unsurprisingly, then, the king is deeply unsettled by the rumors of Jesus that reach him. Theories are floated: John the Baptist raised from the dead (and this before Jesus says anything of his own Resurrection, even to his disciples), Elijah, or a prophet like one of the prophets of old. Herod in a panic agrees with the first theory, probably out of guilt and fear.

Of these theories, the Malachi prophecy best supports Jesus-as-Elijah. Jesus' own activities would lend further credence to the Elijah theory. When he raised Jairus's daughter from the dead, the crowds would remember how Elijah raised the widow of Zarephath's son, an account that stresses how "the LORD listened to the voice of Elijah" (I Kings 17:22). Luke places the raising of both the son of the widow of Nain and the daughter of Jairus shortly before Herod's perplexity over Jesus' identity and the Transfiguration itself. So there was every reason, when thinking of Jesus, to have Elijah on the brain.

But for our purposes, the chief point here is that while both John the Baptist and Elijah are candidates for *Jesus'* identity, at this point neither of them is a candidate for *each other's* identity! John, Elijah, and "the prophets" all belong to the same broad category of holy men of God, but no closer identification among them has emerged. The Gospel of John leaves it at that, with the Baptizer denying outright that he is the Christ *or* Elijah *or* one of the prophets, end of discussion (John 1:19–21).

A more or less identical list of candidates is trotted out by the disciples when Jesus asks who people think he is. "John the Baptist; and others say, Elijah; and others, one of the prophets" (Mark 8:28). Same as before: John and Elijah both might be aligned with Jesus, but the two are not aligned with each other. Peter's marvelous progress in this moment is to set Jesus apart from the category of holy men of God into a category all his own: "You are the Christ" (8:29).

So when, at the Transfiguration, Elijah makes an appearance, it's as much as anything to confirm that Elijah and Jesus are *not* one and the same. If there is a new-Elijah, Jesus is not he.

By the same token, Jesus is not a new-Moses, either. But there seems to have been less confusion about that overall.

Afterwards, the three disciples who witnessed the Transfiguration are still trying to work out its implications—and if changing the subject allows them to avoid the touchy subject of the cross, so much the better. It's easy to assume their query about Elijah was code language for John. But as we've seen, so far John and Elijah haven't been linked.

More likely, the disciples' question is about the Elijah *they just saw*, who did come, at least to the mountaintop, and yet obviously did *not* restore all things. But if the messenger of the covenant and the Christ are supposed to restore all things, and Jesus is the Christ, but the Christ is *not* Elijah old or new... well, it's enough to give anyone a full-blown scribal headache. How do you make all the pieces fit together?

It's only now that *Jesus* makes the explicit connection between John and Elijah. He decisively sets aside any lingering imputation of the new-Elijah status to himself and lays it firmly on John. "But I tell you that Elijah has come, and they did to him whatever they pleased" (9:13). Those who have ears to hear, let them hear: Jesus means John the Baptist, beheaded at Herod's command after a frivolous vow.

What this further means is that restoration is *not* new-Elijah's chief task. Suffering is. As it is written of Elijah, so also of the Son of Man, to "suffer many things and be treated with contempt" (9:12).

So even changing the subject to Elijah can't rescue the disciples from the inevitability of the cross.

Matthew develops the association of John with Elijah more fully. He reports a story that doesn't appear in Mark, where John's disciples are sent by their master in prison to inquire whether Jesus is the one to come, or if they should look for another.

It is, truly, an astonishing question. How could John *not* know? Jesus sends back the answer that the blind see, the lame walk, the lepers are cleansed, the deaf hear, the dead are raised, the poor hear good news, "and blessed is the one who is not offended by me" (Matthew 11:6). John, apparently, is offended, or tempted to be offended. Did *he* take Jesus to be the new-Elijah who would refine, launder, burn, and tread?

Afterwards Jesus turns his attention on the crowds who gawked at John yet failed to hear his message. Jesus confirms that John is a prophet, "and more than a prophet" (11:9). John *is* the messenger of Malachi, "and if you are willing to accept it, he is Elijah who is to come" (11:14).

Still, this is less of a compliment than it might appear. Maybe that's the crowds' fault: they are too happy with the blazing messenger and not happy enough about the Christ. Jesus adds the startling conclusion, "Among those born of women there has arisen no one greater than John the Baptist. Yet the one who is least in the kingdom of heaven is greater than he" (11:11).

Luke has his own way of connecting John to Elijah, and putting both in their place. He alone records a birth narrative for John. It sets expectations extremely high. After all, it's a familiar phenomenon for God to give a child to the childless in order for that child to go on to do great things, as with Hannah and Elkanah's baby Samuel.

As the angel explains to Zechariah, his and Elizabeth's child will be a Nazirite like Samson the judge, set apart and avoiding strong drink. Better still, this child "will be filled with the Holy Spirit" (1:15)! At the apex of all the promises, the angel announces, "And he will turn many of the children of Israel to the Lord their God, and he will go before him in the spirit and power of Elijah, to turn the hearts of the fathers to the children, and the disobedient to the wisdom of the just, to make ready for the Lord a people prepared" (1:16–17).

It could not be clearer. Right from the start, Luke wants you to see that *John* is the new-Elijah prophesied by Malachi. And at the exact same time, Luke is setting you up.

Luke wants you to be satisfied at first with John-as-Elijah, in order to startle you with the witness of fetal John in Elizabeth's womb, leaping with joy at the coming of the Lord. Do not be content with Elijah alone! He is, after all, only the messenger. After the messenger comes the Lord of hosts.[9]

The christological point has been made. Jesus is not the messenger of the Lord of hosts, but the one who comes after the messenger: the Lord of hosts himself.

According to fourth-century church father John Chrysostom, that's why Elijah's appearance was so necessary to shoring up the christological claim. "Elijah was 'jealous for God's glory,' and would not himself have stood by submissively if Jesus were opposed to God, and said he was God, making himself equal to the Father, yet were not what he said he was."[10]

Jesus makes plain the association of eschatological Elijah with John the Baptist, and both as figures of suffering, not restoration.

But this conversation takes place in private. Only Peter, James, and John are privy to the insight. We have no knowledge as to whether it was shared with the rest of the disciples.

So confusion about who is who, exactly, seems to have continued—the eschatological-Elijah theory about Jesus carrying on unchecked and living a life of its own for some time.

In fact, we see the misattribution again before Mark's Gospel reaches its end. Jesus on the cross utters the horrified cry, "*Eloi, Eloi, lema sabachthani?*" (15:34). This is the Aramaic version of the opening verse of Psalm 22: "My God, my God, why you have you forsaken me?"

The bystanders either don't know their Aramaic or don't know their Psalms. They take Jesus' cry for God to be a cry for Elijah instead—*Eloi* mistaken for "Elijah." Though if you were expecting Elijah to restore all things as the advance guard of the Lord of hosts, it's not a bad guess.

Failing to hear this agonized prayer for what it is, they offer Jesus sour wine on a stick. Lovers of a lurid spectacle, they hope to attract an apocalyptic spectacle as well. As if a drop of liquid could prolong a crucified man's life just long enough to summon a superstar from the past.

Little do they know that certain of those standing there had already seen Elijah, and he did nothing to forestall the cross.

Elijah does not come. Jesus dies. Elijah not only didn't restore all things. He didn't restore Jesus, either.

Shall we hope for better things from Moses? Or does he, too, point toward the cross?

28 Amen I say to you all
that there are certain ones of those standing here,
the same ones will no way, no how taste death
until they should have seen
the Son of Man
coming in his kingdom.

1 And after six days
Jesus takes along
Peter and James and John his brother,
and he bears them up
to a high mountain
by themselves.

2 And he was transfigured
in front of them,

and his face shone like the sun,
while his clothes came to be white like light.

3 And behold
to them appeared
Moses and Elijah
talking together with him.

4 But Peter
speaking up
said to Jesus,
Lord,
it is good for us to be here;
if you wish,
I will make here three tabernacles,
one for you and
one for Moses and
one for Elijah.

5 Him still speaking
behold
a bright cloud
overshadowed them,
and behold
a voice from the cloud
saying:

This is my Son,
the beloved,
in whom I take pleasure;
listen to him.

6 And having heard,
the disciples fell on their faces
and were exceedingly frightened.

7 And Jesus approached
and fastening on to them said,
Be raised and fear not.

8 But lifting up their eyes
they saw nobody
except Jesus himself alone.

9 And them descending
from the mountain
Jesus commanded them, saying:

Tell the vision
to not one single person
until when
the Son of Man
should be raised from the dead.

Exodus : Moses

Matthew and Luke rearrange Jesus' historic companions on the moun-taintop. Moses slides to the front, Elijah to the back. Chronological order has been restored.

Not that Mark ever intended any disrespect to Moses. His order-ing may have been a case of save-the-best-for-last anyway. More importantly, Mark's depiction of the Transfiguration leaves you in no doubt about its Old Testament antiphons. If you're not seeing, hearing, and smelling Mount Sinai all through this story, you're not paying attention.

But for Luke, giving Moses primacy of place is not enough. He goes Mark and Matthew one better. Luke alone of the Evangelists tells you what, precisely, Moses and Elijah were there to talk over with Jesus.

Unfortunately, in this instance, English translations have a habit of concealing more than they reveal, which certainly cuts against the grain of the Transfiguration's purpose.

The King James Version overinterprets, saying they "spake of his *decease* which he should accomplish at Jerusalem." Among recent translations, the habitually paraphrasing NIV, the typically tin-eared and mealy-mouthed NRSV, and the otherwise fidelious ESV all im-prove on "decease," but only with "departure."[11]

Talk about losing the plot! Here's a literal and, in the case of one word, transliterating translation of Luke 9:30–31: "And behold two men were talking together to him, these same were Moses and Elijah, who appearing in glory were speaking of his exodus which he was about to fulfill in Jerusalem."

Exodus! With this one word, we know what kind of story we're dealing with. With this one word, Jesus' Passion predictions snap into sense and focus.

This one word forecasts the expansion in meaning of all that is to come: not only the festival of unleavened bread, not only the shed-ding of the blood of the firstborn lamb, but also a deliverance-escape-exit-exodus from death and the tomb, through and in between the watery graves of Red Sea chaos, out the other side to everlasting life in the promised land of the kingdom of God. The exodus of the children of Israel will be repeated on a cosmic scale.

But let's not get ahead of ourselves. For now, we are not on our way to Jerusalem, or spectators to a grisly sight outside its walls, or rising early on the first day of the week, spices in hand. For now we are on the mountain of Transfiguration, and there is more than enough to talk about right here.

Back in the book of Exodus, Moses is always going up the mountain. Sometimes he brings company. At the outset of chapter 24, he takes three named companions up the mountain with him—Aaron, Nadab, and Abihu—much as Jesus will take three named companions up the mountain with him—Peter, James, and John.

Jesus, however, leaves the crowd behind, while Moses, with the Lord's permission, brings a crowd halfway up. Seventy elders of Israel join the special four to celebrate the covenant, and "they saw the God of Israel" (24:10).

This seems to surprise the narrator, or the narrator assumes it will surprise hearers and readers, for the further point is made: "And [God] did not lay his hand on the chief men of the people of Israel; they beheld God, and ate and drank" (24:11). In other words: believe it or not, *they didn't die!*

What precise manner of beholding is not specified. But, as we'll find out soon enough, there's seeing God... and then there's *seeing* God.

After the feast ends, the Lord summons Moses farther up the mountain. Joshua may or may not accompany him. Aaron and Hur stay behind to moderate disputes. Nobody seems to have realized just yet how much trouble unsupervised Israelites can get into.

"Then Moses went up on the mountain, and the cloud covered the mountain. The glory of the LORD dwelt on Mount Sinai, and the cloud covered it six days. And on the seventh day he called to Moses out of the midst of the cloud" (24:15-16).

So much to discuss! Moses, mountain, cloud, glory.

But let's start with "six days."

Here's the setup for the Transfiguration in Mark's rendering, which Matthew closely follows.

On the way to Caesarea Philippi, Jesus asks his disciples who people think he is. They correctly dispense with the John-, Elijah-, and prophet-theories. Peter proposes by contrast the correct theory: "You are the Christ."

Jesus promptly accepts, but then extends the office of Messiah to include suffering and death. After a tussle with Peter over this painful point, Jesus concludes, "For whoever is ashamed of me and of my words in this adulterous and sinful generation, of him will the Son of Man also be ashamed when he comes in the glory of his Father with the holy angels" (Mark 8:38).

Hold the *Father* part in your mind for later.

Jesus then adds a further remark: "Amen I say to you all that there are certain ones of those standing here, the same ones will no way, no how taste death until they should have seen the kingdom of God having come in power" (9:1).

The chapter-and-versification of the Bible obscures the fact that 9:1 is the hinge between two halves of a continuous story. Lectionaries leave it out of the Transfiguration reading from Mark (likewise the parallel verse in Matthew and Luke). The verse dangles, abandoned and alone, as if it doesn't follow immediately and logically from the discussion of Christhood and suffering and glory, as if it doesn't deliberately foreshadow the about-to-unfold Transfiguration.

But that's exactly what Mark wants you to grasp. Jesus is not Elijah nor John nor one of the prophets but the Christ, that is, the suffering Christ who will be glorified and who in this very way of suffering and being glorified will bring in the kingdom of God.

Jesus' promise that "certain ones of those standing here" will see the kingdom of God coming in power, *but in the mode of the soon-to-be-suffering Christ*, is exactly what will be unveiled on the mountain of Transfiguration.

Which takes place... after six days.

Recall the Exodus account: the cloud covered Mount Sinai for six days. And on the seventh day, that is, on the day *after six days* had elapsed, God called to Moses out of the cloud.

If you hearken further back, the seventh day signifies the day of rest after creation, and the Sabbath every seventh day thereafter.

If you hearken further forward, the seventh day signifies Jesus' deathly rest in the tomb.

Ergo, by these six- and seventh-day associations, Mark is telling you that you don't get glory without hiddenness, resurrection without death, or the kingdom of God without suffering. The one entails the other.

While Moses stands enveloped in God's glory at the peak of Mount Sinai, he receives the law, and in detail. Most of the details concern the meeting places between God and humanity: the ark of the covenant, the tabernacle, the oil lamps, the altar, the robed priests, the Sabbath. This is not the place for the "moral law" of right and wrong, but the specific, tangible, and artistically pleasing crossroads of the divine with the human.

At the end of it, "[God] gave to Moses, when he had finished speaking with him on Mount Sinai, the two tablets of the testimony, tablets of stone, written with the finger of God" (Exodus 31:18).

And then—immediately—everything goes to hell.

Golden calf, stiff-necked people, wrath burning hot, reluctant relenting, smashing of tablets.

Not accidentally, as soon as Jesus returns from the mountain of Transfiguration to the plain, the very first thing he encounters is the abject failure of his disciples to cast out a demon. Not for lack of power; for lack of prayer. "O faithless generation, how long am I to be with you? How long am I to bear with you?" (Mark 9:19).

Moses would appreciate the sentiment. The outcome of the golden calf episode is that the people of Israel have to move on from Mount Sinai. They've worn out their welcome. They, too, must return to the plain and the very human struggles that unfold there.

Before they go, Moses makes a last daring request of a severely displeased God: "Show me your glory" (Exodus 33:18).

The Lord responds with one of his most remarkable speeches in all of Scripture. "I will make all my goodness pass before you and will proclaim before you my name 'The LORD.' And I will be gracious to whom I will be gracious, and will show mercy on whom I will show mercy. But you cannot see my face, for man shall not see me and live. Behold, there is a place by me where you shall stand on the rock, and while my glory passes by I will put you in a cleft of the rock, and I will cover you with my hand until I have passed by. Then I will take away my hand, and you shall see my back, but my face shall not be seen" (33:19–23).

After the massive disaster of covenant gone wrong, God himself extends and elaborates on his holy name: not only I AM WHO I AM, but also I WILL BE GRACIOUS TO WHOM I WILL BE GRACIOUS and I WILL SHOW MERCY ON WHOM I WILL SHOW MERCY. In this setting, he consents for his glory, though still not his face, to be seen.

Which is a fair indication that grace and mercy, in all their glory, are hard to bear.

In the Gospel story, the pattern is reversed. All along, the disciples have been seeing Jesus' face. It is a human face; you can look upon it and live. But when after six days they ascend the mountain, for the first time they behold Jesus' glory.

In the time that remains to Moses on the mountain, he receives a new pair of tablets to replace the smashed ones. He hears the covenant reaffirmed and the promised land repromised. He is charged again with the observance of the feast of unleavened bread, that potent reminder of the exodus from Egypt.

Likewise, the Lord reminds Moses of the cost of the exodus, not only to Pharaoh and the Egyptians back then, but now and in the future to Moses and the Israelites: "All that open the womb are mine, all your male livestock, the firstborn of cow and sheep. The firstborn of a donkey you shall redeem with a lamb, or if you will not redeem it you shall break its neck. All the firstborn of your sons you shall redeem" (Exodus 34:19–20).

It is a cost, and a redemption, that God is setting himself up to pay, one day, far into the future.

While all this is happening, forty days and forty nights elapse, during which Moses eats no bread and drinks no water. Mountain or desert—either way, you go hungry.

But while Jesus comes out famished from his forty days in the wild places of God, Moses comes out radiant. One might almost say, transfigured. "When Moses came down from Mount Sinai, with the two tablets of the testimony in his hand as he came down from the mountain, Moses did not know that the skin of his face shone because he had been talking with God. Aaron and all the people of Israel saw Moses, and behold, the skin of his face shone, and they were afraid to come near him. But Moses called to them... And when Moses had finished speaking with them, he put a veil over his face" (34:29–31a, 33).

For all his Moses and Sinai allusions, Mark won't quite go this far. According to him, it's only Jesus' clothes that shine. Matthew goes all-in on the Moses comparison, Luke hedges, but both agree that the face of Jesus, like the face of Moses, is changed.

Whether it's the clothing alone or the face as well, all three Synoptic brothers agree on this: Jesus' Transfiguration points not only to the power of God or the approval of God, but above all to the glory of God.

Which brings us, by a winding path down the mountain, through Damascus, and onward to Corinth and Rome, to an appointment with the apostle Paul.

Paul's Epistles are famously modest where biographical details of Jesus are concerned. Death by crucifixion, check. Resurrection from the dead, check. Both in abundance. Nearly everything else is missing, at least explicitly. We can infer that Paul could infer the familiarity of his letter-recipients with the story of Jesus. The apostle's job was not to tell them what happened, but to help them grasp what it meant, about God first of all, about themselves second.

So it's not exactly surprising that Paul makes no open reference to Christ's mountaintop meta*morph*osis. But Paul is obsessed with Christ's *morphḗ*—the form that can be transformed, the figure that can be transfigured. And if Christ's *morphḗ*, then by extension ours, too.

In Galatians, Paul describes himself as having the birthpangs of a spiritual mother in speaking to "my little children, for whom I am again in the anguish of childbirth until Christ is formed [*morphōthê̄*] in you!" (4:19).

This same language of form or figure, *morphê̄*, is all over Philippians, starting with the famous Christ hymn: "Have this mind among yourselves, which is yours in Christ Jesus, who, though he was in the form [*morphê̄*] of God, did not count equality with God a thing to be grasped" (2:5–6).

Paul being Paul, he reminds the Philippians how it's only by faith that they acquire the *morphê̄* of Christ. It's worth following the whole logic that surrounds the key term here. "For his sake I have suffered the loss of all things and count them as rubbish, in order that I may gain Christ and be found in him, not having a righteousness of my own that comes from the law, but that which comes through faith in Christ, the righteousness from God that depends on faith—that I may know him and the power of his resurrection, and may share his sufferings, becoming like him [*symmorphizómenos*] in his death, that by any means possible I may attain the resurrection from the dead" (3:8–11).

The English "becoming like him" obscures the underlying term with *morphê̄* hiding inside of it. The word means something like having-a-form-with, being-configured-to. The *sym-* prefix in Greek, like the *con-* prefix in Latin, means "with." In Paul's logic, by faith I receive the form of Christ and am thereby with him, which means suffering and death in order to gain resurrection and life.

A bit later in the same chapter Paul speaks again of the Lord Jesus Christ who "will transform [*metaschēmatísei*] the body of our humiliation that it may be conformed [*sýmmorphon*] to the body of his glory" (Philippians 3:21).[12] "Transform" in this sentence doesn't have the *morphê̄* root but another one that will be familiar to English speakers, *schêma*, meaning "shape."

To paraphrase inelegantly, Christ will transschematize the shape of our humiliated bodies by configuring them to his own glorious body.

It's easy to get distracted by etymological parlor tricks. The point is that the body—Moses's, Jesus', ours—is the intended recipient of

God's glory. Glory in the form of resurrection is promised, but not apart from suffering and death.

Paul reiterates the promise in Romans 8:29–30. "For those whom [God] foreknew he also predestined to be conformed [*symmórphous*] to the image of his Son, in order that he might be the firstborn among many brothers. And those whom he predestined he also called, and those whom he called he also justified, and those whom he justified he also glorified." Sharing in the *morphḗ* of Christ ultimately leads to being glorified by God.

So Paul speaks of *morphḗ* and *sýmmorphos*, Christ's and ours. The question is, does he ever speak of metamorphosis?

Yes. Twice. But not Christ's! In Paul's letters, Christ's glory is *not* linked to Christ's metamorphosis. When Paul deploys the word, it's with a different intent from Mark and Matthew. He uses the notion of metamorphosis only to talk about something that will happen to *us*.

Romans 12:2 mirrors the other instances of Paul's *morphḗ-*language. "Do not be conformed [*syschēmatízesthe*] to this world, but be transformed [*metamorphoûsthe*] by the renewal of your mind, that by testing you may discern what is the will of God, what is good and acceptable and perfect." In the first term the synonym *schêma* lies at the root, rather than *morphḗ*. Here as in Philippians 3:21, the variation in terminology is probably a matter of good literary style. But in the second clause we have one of the two instances where Paul uses the whole metamorphosis compound, in the form of a passive imperative: *Metamorphoûsthe!* "Be metamorphosed!"

The religiously ambitious love to co-opt the language of "transfiguration" into a spiritual self-improvement program. It turns into a get-good-quick scheme, an overrealized eschatology for human perfectibility. Scout for books, meditations, or prayers on the Transfiguration, and you'll find a lot about *you*, not so much about Christ.

But Paul does theology with his verbs as much as with his prepositions. His challenge is right there in *metamorphoûsthe*. The irony of a passive imperative is that the very person to whom it is addressed *cannot* bring it about!

And if your christology is still shaky after all this time, you might be unprepared for the still more startling point: even *Jesus* did not bring about his own Transfiguration. He, in the passive voice, *was* transfigured.

By whom? That is the question the cloud has to answer. We'll get there in due course.

But as for us and our being transfigured, the answer was already unveiled in Romans 8, where Paul spoke of our being conformed to the image of God's Son immediately after his extended meditation on the work of the Spirit.

Paul's point as well as his passive verb resound again in II Corinthians 3:18. "And we all, unveiling the face, beholding-as-in-a-mirror the glory of the Lord, are being transfigured [*metamorphoúmetha*] into his image, from glory unto glory, even as from Lord Spirit."[13]

Time for some more etymological fun and games. The root of the word "unveiling," *anakekalumménō*, has the same *kalyp* as in *apokálypsis*, "apocalypse," "revelation," or "uncovering." What was hidden is now disclosed. You are seeing your own face properly for the first time by gazing into a mirror that doesn't reflect back your own image, but the image of the Lord's glory in your own face. The word for image here is *eikóna*, "icon."

So, your being metamorphosed is your movement from having a concealed, hidden, veiled face to having an open, beaming, glorious face, making you an icon of Christ. And this by the power of the Spirit. Here, as in Romans 8, we have an all-out trinitarian extravaganza of salvation.

Yet this verse from II Corinthians 3 is just the tip of the iceberg. It appears halfway through what I'll venture to call Paul's commentary on the Transfiguration of Christ.

It unfolds, of course, in Paul's characteristic theological key, without mention of Elijah or Peter, James, and John—akin to how Paul can talk about the incarnation of Christ without ever mentioning Mary, Gabriel, or Bethlehem, or the death of Christ without ever mentioning Judas, Pontius Pilate, or Golgotha.

Paul starts out by appealing to the Corinthian believers themselves as "a letter from Christ delivered by us, written not with ink but with the Spirit of the living God, not on tablets of stone but on tablets of human hearts" (3:3). In short, Paul begins his Transfiguration commentary with a trinitarian theophany calling to mind Mount Sinai with its tablets of stone.

Inconclusive? Keep going. "Now if the ministry of death, carved in letters on stone, came with such glory that the Israelites could not gaze at Moses's face because of its glory, which was being brought to an end, will not the ministry of the Spirit have even more glory?" (3:7–8).

Tablets of stone, glory, Moses's shining face: all the same allusions that the Synoptic Transfiguration accounts make to Exodus.

Paul then interprets the veil over Moses's face, shielding the Israelites from a glory they can't handle, as a metaphor for the failure to grasp Jesus as the Christ. The veil is an impediment to true beholding and understanding, but it can be removed by the power of the Spirit, who alone grants the freedom to behold and understand.

Exactly here is where Paul speaks of our unveiled faces being transfigured, *metamorphoúmetha*, through beholding the glory of the Lord as a work of the Spirit.

On the other side of believers' unfolding metamorphosis, Paul asserts that we ought not lose heart. "Even if our gospel is veiled, it is veiled to those who are perishing. In their case the god of this world has blinded the minds of the unbelievers, to keep them from seeing the light of the gospel of the glory of Christ, who is the image of God" (4:4).

Note how light has become the central motif: the light of glory, the glory of Christ, Christ the image or rather icon of God. "For God, who said, 'Let light shine out of darkness,' has shone in our hearts to give the light of the knowledge of the glory of God in the face of Jesus Christ" (4:6).

The light of glory in the *face* of Jesus Christ! How can Paul *not* be alluding to the Transfiguration?

And if that still doesn't convince you, wait till he gets to tabernacles!

However, as we are about to learn, it is extremely important not to rush to tabernacles too soon. The light of glory in the face of the transfigured Jesus can blind rather than enlighten. Before there can be tabernacles, there must be a Passover.

For is glory all of the same kind? Or is one kind of glory different from another?

Tabernacles : Israel

When you're plunged into a new situation, you make sense of it by aligning it with some story you already know. If you know the story, then you know how to act and how things will turn out.

But you have to be sure you've identified the new story correctly. Operate according to Beauty and the Beast when you're really in Little Red Riding Hood, and it will turn out even worse for you than it did for the little girl who ended up inside a wolf's belly.

If you're a Christian reader, looking back on the Gospels with the benefit of hindsight and apostolic witness, you see Moses and therefore think exodus, which in turn puts you in mind of Passover, which in turn tells you which exact story Jesus is headed into. You can therefore act accordingly, knowing how it will turn out. (Maybe.)

But Peter in this new situation doesn't think of the exodus or Passover. Not at all. Not even with the benefit of eavesdropping. Plunged into the unprecedented, Peter grasps and grabs and turns up tabernacles.

Passover has so entirely, and understandably, overtaken the mind of the church for interpreting Jesus that we forget—or never even notice—the Feast of Tabernacles, Sukkot in Hebrew. It's sometimes also called the Festival of Ingathering, since it takes place in the autumn after the harvest is in.

Exodus is the first book of the Bible to talk about Tabernacles, and in fact does so right before Moses and the seventy meet God face to face. Tabernacles appears together with the two other key festivals of the year, Unleavened Bread (i.e., Passover, in Hebrew Pesach) and Harvest (i.e., Weeks, in Hebrew Shavuot and in Greek Pentecost). "Three times in the year you shall keep a feast to me. You shall keep the *Feast of Unleavened Bread*. As I commanded you, you shall eat unleavened bread for seven days at the appointed time in the month of Abib, for in it you came out of Egypt. None shall appear before me empty-handed. You shall keep the *Feast of Harvest*, of the firstfruits of your labor, of what you sow in the field. You shall keep the *Feast of Ingathering* at the end of the year, when you gather in from the field the fruit of your labor. Three times in the year shall all your males appear before the Lord GOD" (23:14–16).

The details of these three festivals are further elaborated in Exodus 34, the same chapter in which Moses beholds the backside of God's glory. "You shall keep the *Feast of Unleavened Bread*. Seven days you shall eat unleavened bread, as I commanded you, at the time appointed in the month Abib, for in the month Abib you came out from Egypt. All that open the womb are mine, all your male livestock, the firstborn of cow and sheep. The firstborn of a donkey you shall redeem with a lamb, or if you will not redeem it you shall break its neck. All the firstborn of your sons you shall redeem. And none shall appear before me empty-handed. Six days you shall work, but on the seventh day you shall rest. In plowing time and in harvest you shall rest. You shall observe the *Feast of Weeks*, the firstfruits of wheat harvest, and the *Feast of Ingathering* at the year's end. Three times in the year shall all your males appear before the LORD God, the God of Israel. For I will cast out nations before you and enlarge your borders; no one shall covet your land, when you go up to appear before the LORD your God three times in the year" (34:18–24).

The first thing to notice is that males are put on notice. Many in our day and age have regretted the much rarer appearance of females in the biblical narrative, and fair enough. But in the biblical world, to be male, and worse yet a firstborn male, is a dangerous condition, frequently fatal. Females are nearly always spared. Males are treated as spares.[14] Here again God is setting up his firstborn, only-begotten Son for a deadly end.

And second, notice that both Exodus passages hint toward the emergence of Passover, Pentecost, and Tabernacles as pilgrimage festivals. Once the Lord settles into his semi-permanent address in the temple on Mount Zion in Jerusalem, his people will stream in and up to worship and sacrifice before him three times a year.

It makes sense that God's Son would meet his doom during one of these festivals, since he would travel to the city for the occasion.

It also makes sense that God's Spirit would be poured out at another one of these festivals, since so many of the people of God would travel to the city for the occasion.

That accounts for both Passover and Pentecost.

But what about poor neglected Tabernacles?

It didn't start out neglected. In fact, up till Jesus' time at least, Tabernacles was the foremost festival of Israel. Josephus, a Jewish contemporary of the apostles, thought so: "The feast of tabernacles... was celebrated by the Hebrews as a most holy and most eminent feast."[15] Leviticus refers to it once simply as "the feast of the LORD" (23:39) in a chapter that covers all of Israel's festivals—successively Sabbath, Passover, Firstfruits, Pentecost, Trumpets, and Atonement. The list culminates in Tabernacles. This is where we get all the details of the proper observance of Sukkot, as still practiced by faithful Israel to this day. Here is the description in full.

"And the LORD spoke to Moses, saying, 'Speak to the people of Israel, saying, On the fifteenth day of this seventh month and for seven days is the Feast of Booths to the LORD. On the first day shall be a holy convocation; you shall not do any ordinary work. For seven days you shall present food offerings to the LORD. On the eighth day you shall hold a holy convocation and present a food offering to the LORD. It is a solemn assembly; you shall not do any ordinary work.

"'These are the appointed feasts of the LORD, which you shall proclaim as times of holy convocation, for presenting to the LORD food offerings, burnt offerings and grain offerings, sacrifices and drink offerings, each on its proper day, besides the LORD's Sabbaths and besides your gifts and besides all your vow offerings and besides all your freewill offerings, which you give to the LORD.

"'On the fifteenth day of the seventh month, when you have gathered in the produce of the land, you shall celebrate the feast of the LORD seven days. On the first day shall be a solemn rest, and on the eighth day shall be a solemn rest. And you shall take on the first day the fruit of splendid trees, branches of palm trees and boughs of leafy trees and willows of the brook, and you shall rejoice before the LORD your God seven days. You shall celebrate it as a feast to the LORD for seven days in the year. It is a statute forever throughout your generations; you shall celebrate it in the seventh month. You shall dwell in booths for seven days. All native Israelites shall dwell in booths, that your generations may know that I made the people of Israel dwell in booths when I brought them out of the land of Egypt: I am the LORD your God.' Thus Moses declared to the people of Israel the appointed feasts of the LORD" (Leviticus 23:33–44).

Time to sort out some terminology. The common translation of Hebrew *sukkah*, plural *sukkot*, is "booth"—an unmelodious choice for English speakers. It evokes toll charges on the highway, rigged games at the county fair, and Lucy charging "five cents, please" for spurious psychiatric advice. What the word means is a temporary rugged shelter, as in Genesis 33 where Jacob builds *sukkot* for his livestock and accordingly names the place Succoth, otherwise transliterated as Sukkot.

The term "tabernacle" is more evocatively religious, though possibly it evokes more than it ought. Latin translated *sukkah* as *tabernāculum*—whence the English term—meaning simply "tent." Of course, a tent is nothing if not a temporary and often rugged shelter. But you need a bit of inferential stitching to make the leap from the Ingathering festival's short-term booth of branches to the tabernacle where God dwelt among the Israelites before the temple was built. In Hebrew *that* tabernacle is called a *mishkan* (the rabbinic term for God's Presence, Shekinah, is built from the same root), not a *sukkah*.

Or, maybe all you need is the Septuagint. There the necessary linguistic leap has already been made: whether *sukkah*-booth or *mishkan*-tabernacle, both words get translated into Greek as *skēnḗ*, "tent."

That was not due to either impoverished vocabulary or outright presumption. The alignment of terms is suggested by the Scriptures themselves. In II Samuel 7:6, God responds to David's offer to build him a house. This time the King James Version gets it exactly right: "I have not dwelt in any house since the time that I brought up the children of Israel out of Egypt, even to this day, but have walked in a *tent* and in a *tabernacle*." The Hebrew words are, respectively, *ohel* (the generic term for tent, which pops up all over the Old Testament), and *mishkan*, the freighted word for tabernacle.

The Greek, in turn, makes these words to be respectively *katálu-ma*, an inn (like the kind Mary and Joseph get turned away from in Luke 2:7, and the one where Jesus enjoys his last supper in Mark 14:14 and Luke 22:11), and *skēnḗ*, the generic Greek word for tent, which often translates *ohel*. For example, Jacob's *sukkah*, "booth," for livestock (Genesis 33:17) and *ohel*, "tent," for himself (Genesis 33:19) both show up in the Septuagint as *skēnḗ*.

Which means that, despite other options, in II Samuel 7 the Septuagint lines up Hebrew *mishkan*-tabernacle with Greek *skēnḗ*-tent. This will prove extremely fertile soil for the Greek-speaking and -writing authors of the New Testament. We'll return to this later.

But first, a few more items to extract from Leviticus. We have another covert exodus here. In Leviticus 23:36, what is translated into English as "solemn assembly" appears in the Septuagint's Greek as *exódión*, exodus. That usage turns up again in Numbers 29:35, in an extended passage that also details Sukkot observance, but this time with reference to the daily tally of animals to sacrifice.

This translation would seem to be another fertile liberty of the Septuagint, since the Hebrew behind it, *atsarah*, simply means "assembly," as in a gathering of people to worship. But since rest from labor is commanded—"you shall not do any work"—the translation as exodus points to the deliverance from the burdens of work on the day of solemn assembly. Not such a liberty, after all.

More to the point, we have an *overt* exodus in the Leviticus account of Tabernacles. Here at last we get the reason for the festival's name. "All native Israelites shall dwell in booths, that your generations may know that I made the people of Israel dwell in booths when I brought them out of the land of Egypt: I am the LORD your God" (23:42–43). Passover buys you the time, and buys you back your sons, to get out of Egypt before death strikes. Passover sends you across the Red Sea, into the wilderness, over to Mount Sinai. But Tabernacles is the celebration of your accomplished and acquired freedom, of the success of the exodus rather than of the exodus itself.

Last but not least, among the plants specified for the celebration are palm branches. They still appear in the bundle of *lulavim* waved in

Sukkot services in the synagogue today. Which is why, when pilgrims to Jerusalem saw Jesus and immediately thought of him in terms of Sukkot and tabernacles, they laid down palm branches before him. If the mood is joy, and the one being joyfully acclaimed has consistently delivered the sick and possessed out of their own personal Egypts, then yes, Sukkot is the right festival to choose. It is merrymaking *after* the hard work has been done, *after* the harvest has come in.

And that's the problem. Nobody wants to hear they're not yet at Sukkot, but right in the middle of Passover—much less what part Jesus will have to play in Passover's dramatic reenactment.

Deuteronomy repeats a shortened form of the instructions for the Feast of Tabernacles (16:13–17). It also extends the celebration to everyone in your midst: "You and your son and your daughter, your male servant and your female servant, the Levite, the sojourner, the fatherless, and the widow who are within your towns" (16:14). The mission to the Gentiles is foreshadowed right here, with a universal merrymaking at the completed ingathering of the nations.

Later in Deuteronomy, one more key feature is attached to Tabernacles observance, but only every seventh year, the sabbath year. In that year, "during the Festival of Booths, when all Israel comes to appear before the LORD your God at the place that he will choose, you shall read this law before all Israel in their hearing. Assemble the people—men, women, and children, as well as the aliens residing in your towns—so that they may hear and learn to fear the LORD your God and to observe diligently all the words of this law" (31:10–12). This is a miniature and ritualized renewal of the covenant.

It's no surprise, then, that Sukkot also becomes the occasion for irregular, charismatic, and dramatic renewals of the covenant.

Solomon selected the Feast of Tabernacles as the occasion for the consecration of the temple—another reason, perhaps, for aligning the *sukkah*-booth with the *mishkan*-tabernacle in the Septuagint.[16]

Not by accident, at the heart of the new temple sits the ark of the covenant containing the two tablets of stone that Moses received at Mount Horeb/Sinai. Moses is mentioned many times in Solomon's long prayer, which features continual pleas for God to hear the cries of his people, in the form of if-then propositions. For example, "If they pray toward this place and acknowledge your name and turn from their sin... then hear in heaven and forgive the sin of your servants" (I Kings 8:35–36).

All of Solomon's petitions are prefaced by one gigantic metaphysical question: "But will God indeed dwell on the earth?" (8:27).

The answer comes swiftly. When God descends to take possession, "a cloud filled the house of the LORD, so that the priests could not stand to minister because of the cloud, for the glory of the LORD filled the house of the LORD" (8:10–11). Note the motifs: tabernacle, cloud, glory.

Such an affirmation of God's willingness to dwell on earth made the destruction of Solomon's temple centuries later all the harder to bear. It also made the rebuilding of the temple after the exile all the more urgent. Nehemiah thus made use of Sukkot to renew the covenant when the Israelites returned from Babylon.

The exiles have come back to a home that has never been their home; they know it only from Psalms and their grandparents' laments. Within the rebuilt walls of Jerusalem, they gather with Ezra the scribe and knuckle down to Torah study. It just so happens to be the seventh month.

"And they found it written in the Law that the LORD had commanded by Moses that the people of Israel should dwell in booths during the feast of the seventh month, and that they should proclaim it and publish it in all their towns and in Jerusalem, 'Go out to the hills and bring branches of olive, wild olive, myrtle, palm, and other leafy trees to make booths, as it is written'" (Nehemiah 8:14–15).

They do exactly that, "each on his roof, and in their courts and in the courts of the house of God, and in the square at the Water Gate and in the square at the Gate of Ephraim" (8:16). As far as they can tell, they're the first generation since Joshua to observe the festival. Maybe Solomon's upstaging of the Lord's festival with his fancy new temple didn't count.

After seven days of tabernacling, "on the eighth day there was a solemn assembly"—here again, an *exódion*, exodus—"according to the rule" (8:18).

Speaking of the eighth day...

Remember the discussion about why the Transfiguration took place "after six days," that is, on the seventh day? Because Moses ascended Mount Sinai on the seventh day; because the Sabbath falls on the seventh day; because Jesus lies in the tomb on the seventh day?

All excellent explanations. Except that Luke disagrees.

In his account, Jesus climbs the mountain "about eight days after these sayings" (9:28) concerning how certain of them would not taste death before they saw the kingdom of God.

Synoptic discrepancies have grieved interpreters for centuries. Harmonizings have been the result. The last great Eastern church father, John of Damascus, saw here two different conventions for counting. "Those, then, who said 'after six days' subtracted the end-units—I mean the first and the last days—and counted those in the middle; but he who counted eight days included middle and end in his number. People are used to counting either one way or the other."[17] Modern scholars often take this approach as well. Both "after six days" and "about eight days after" can easily be reduced to "a week or so later."

Of course, if that's all it means, why go to the trouble of changing it? You can grasp Luke's reasons for wanting to emphasize, say, the alteration in Jesus' face as opposed to just his clothes, as Mark has it, or for wanting to delete the word "metamorphosed" altogether, despite both Mark and Matthew vouching for it, because it would strike his own audience the wrong way. But surely there's nothing at stake in how you count up the days of a week!

Which brings us to a key hermeneutical principle: biblical numbers are neither math nor a secret code. This is why every calculated prediction of the end of the world and the population of heaven is wrong, wrong, wrong.

Biblical numbers are neither math nor code, but they are most definitely symbolic. If Luke changes the number, it's not because he calculates or codes differently. It's because he wants to shift the symbol.

Throughout the Old Testament, almost every invocation of "six days" refers to creation and the working week. The only exceptions are the ascent of Moses to the mountaintop, the days of the feast of unleavened bread, and the period of marching around Jericho before the attack. Correlative to these six-day periods are seventh-day Sabbaths, culminations of festivals, and priestly examinations of the progression of an illness and its healing.

But an eighth day is a paradigm-wrecker. On the eighth day you have busted out of the rhythm of the week and the cycle of historical time. If you are a priest of Israel, the eighth day is the day for costly sacrifices, circumcisions, and ordinations. If you are a church father, the eighth day is a specific Sunday, not the first day of creation when God created light and declared it good, but the Sunday after the Saturday of death and the tomb, when God called forth his Son and declared him alive.

But above all, the eighth day is the last day of Sukkot, the day of the solemn assembly or exodus, observed by Jews still as Shemini Atzeret, which simply means "eighth day of assembly." "On the eighth day you shall hold a holy convocation and present a food offering to the LORD" (Leviticus 23:36; cf. Numbers 29:35). Ezra and company did exactly that (Nehemiah 8:18). Solomon sent the crowds home from the new temple on the eighth day (I Kings 8:66; cf. II Chronicles 7:9). The rededication of the temple under Hezekiah boasts both eight-day and eighth-day observances (II Chronicles 29).

So again we are forced to ask: what story are we in? Is this Passover, or Sukkot?

Luke goes easier on the disciples than Mark does. The latter accuses Peter of being a terrified babbler; the former excuses him with nothing worse than sleepiness. In fact, in Luke, Peter and his pals sleep right through the crucial conversation with Moses and Elijah and therefore miss the key term "exodus" altogether.

Given that, given the appearance of eschatological figures, given the glory bestowed upon Jesus, and given the eighth day on which all this takes place, Luke can hardly blame Peter for thinking he's in a Sukkot story. Peter believes he has busted out of cyclical and historical time and has been swept up into glory. This is the new normal, he reasons. Nail it down while you can.

Yet even Sukkot ends, its temporary shelters dismantled. This is, after all, the eighth day. The festival is nearly over. It's too late to build your *sukkah* now. You shouldn't have been sleeping.

Peter wasn't entirely wrong in his interpretation of events. The Transfiguration is indeed a foretaste of the festival to come—the eschatological Sukkot. But just a foretaste, no more. It will give the disciples the hope they need to carry them through the Passover trials ahead, when something other than temporary shelters gets nailed down. It will orient them toward the ultimate goal at which Passover points.

But you can't jump the line. Passover has to play out fully, and so does Pentecost, before Sukkot's temporary shelters can become permanent.

As Paul the apostle well knew.

Throughout II Corinthians 3 and 4, Paul ruminates expansively on the tablets of stone, Moses's radiant face, the veil of misunderstanding, our being metamorphosed by the Spirit, and the light of glory in the face of Jesus Christ. Paul comments upon the Transfiguration of the Lord by every means except outright historical referent, as he is wont to do.

His argument reaches its culmination in chapter 5, where he speaks of *skēnḗ*, the Greek word that covers *ohel*-tent, *sukkah*-booth, and *mishkan*-tabernacle. Here Paul layers yet another meaning onto the term. "For we know that if the tent that is our earthly home is destroyed, we have a building from God, a house not made with hands, eternal in the heavens. For in this tent we groan, longing to put on our heavenly dwelling, if indeed by putting it on we may not be found naked. For while we are still in this tent, we groan, being burdened—not that we would be unclothed, but that we would be further clothed, so that what is mortal may be swallowed up by life" (5:1–4).

An apt metaphor for a tentmaker by trade! Not to mention someone who had celebrated Sukkot many times. The earthly body is a rugged, temporary, and easily dismantled *sukkah*. Our hope is not for this *sukkah* to be dismantled forever, leaving us even less sheltered than in fragile seasonal booths.

Rather, we hope to be fully sheltered in an everlasting resurrection body—a body such as Jesus' risen body. His Resurrection means that perishable tabernacles will become permanent temples. "He who has prepared us for this very thing is God, who has given us the Spirit as a guarantee" (5:5). But for now, we have to wait it out. We can celebrate an annual Sukkot, but not yet the eschatological one.

If Paul the apostle thinks it essential to discuss the Transfiguration, however allusively; if the Second Epistle of Peter does, too, but explicitly; and if all three Synoptics feature it prominently, then it becomes odd, not to say uncomfortable, that the Gospel of John does *not*.

Or does it?

If you are trained on Jesus' biography in the key of Matthew, Mark, and Luke, it certainly looks like the Transfiguration has been omitted from John. Of course, like the Synoptics, John's Gospel maintains the same basic shape of the Jesus story: beginning with origins, progressing through adulthood, culminating in death, and leaping beyond the bounds of every other biography by continuing the story after death. But there are just enough differences between the Synoptics and John to be jarring.

In John, Jesus has a mother but not a birth. He battles Satan but not in the wilderness or with exorcisms. He receives the Holy Spirit and commissions a baptism but does not get baptized. He gives his flesh to eat and blood to drink but does not institute a Supper. He prays about his imminent demise but not in the Garden of Gethsemane. And although he is glorified, Jesus does not get transfigured on a mountaintop.

But he *does* go to Jerusalem for Sukkot.

One of the most striking of the many striking differences between the Synoptics and John is how often the latter places Jesus in Jerusalem.

The cleansing of the Jerusalem temple *starts* the action in John instead of wrapping it up, and at Passover no less, forming an *inclusio* between the Gospel's beginning and its end. Jesus makes the pilgrimage to Jerusalem again for an unnamed festival in John 5; since all the other festivals are named, we can infer or decide that this must have been Pentecost. In John 10 he goes to Jerusalem for Hanukkah,[18] an act of supererogation if ever there was one, since it was a later development, not mentioned in the Old Testament or mandated as a pilgrimage festival.

And in John 7, Jesus travels to Jerusalem for Sukkot. "Now the Jews' Feast of Booths was at hand" (7:2). In Greek the word is *skēnopēgía*—you can spot the noun *skēnḗ* linked up with the verb *pḗgnumi*, which means "to pitch," as in a tent. This is the only explicit reference to celebrating the festival of Sukkot in the New Testament.

As usual, Jesus' appearance provokes dissension in the crowd. Some say he's a good man, others that he's a deceiver leading the people astray. Even his brothers don't believe in him. Not yet, anyway. The Book of Acts places them with Mary among the company of believers rejoicing at Jesus' Resurrection. But John's Gospel doesn't travel quite that far forward in time.

As the seven days of the festival tick by, Jesus takes the opportunity to teach in the temple, whose destruction he had prophesied along with its rebuilding in three days, meaning his body, not the building itself. His initial remarks focus on glory, Moses, Sabbath, and healing. The first two items are familiar from the Synoptic Transfiguration scene, and the third might be implied by it.

Jesus' sermons conclude, "Do not judge by appearances, but judge with right judgment" (7:24)—which might be easier for the crowds to do if they got to see Jesus transfigured in front of them. But maybe not. Peter didn't do all that well, despite seeing everything.

What then follows is a dispute about whether Jesus can possibly be the Christ, the same discussion that directly precedes the Transfiguration in Mark's Gospel. The Pharisees get roped into the argument and send officers to arrest Jesus. They are met with a riddle about Jesus' imminent departure—"I will be with you a little longer, and then I am going to him who sent me" (John 7:33)—which you might call his exodus.

The crowds aren't asleep, but they still miss the point and imagine Jesus' itinerant ministry will take him to "the Dispersion among the Greeks" so he can "teach the Greeks" (7:35).

All in all, we're looking at a level of incomprehension to rival that of the disciples in Mark.

Then we come to "the last day of the feast, the great day"—which is to say, the eighth day, Shemini Atzeret.

By Jesus' time this day had acquired an additional custom, namely praying for rain. The Mishnah Sukkah, a later rabbinic compilation based on earlier traditions, recalls this rite in Jerusalem. The priests would fill a golden flagon with water from the pool of Siloam (which Jesus will visit in John 9, healing a man blind from birth while he's there). The priests would then process onward to the Water Gate—the same one mentioned in Nehemiah's renewed Sukkot—blow a shofar three times, and pour out the water, linking it prayerfully to the longed-for rain.

The traditional synagogue reading from the Prophets for Sukkot is the fourteenth chapter of Zechariah. Reader be warned: it is horrifying. There is gruesome and gratuitous violence, warfare and deportation, earthquakes and fault lines both geological and political, plagues of rotting flesh, panic and punishment. For such an upbeat festival like Sukkot—Deuteronomy instructs "that you will be altogether joyful" (16:15)—the doomful notes of the prophet jar and jangle.

But at the heart of Zechariah's dark prophecy sound a very few words of hope. On the eschatological day known only to the Lord, "living waters shall flow out of Jerusalem" (14:8). This faint note of optimism probably suggested the water ritual. It's a good verse for drawing water from the pool of Siloam, and a good verse for praying about rain.

Not only the priests of the temple chose to focus on this, of all available motifs, from the Zechariah reading; so did Jesus. It's a good guess that in John 7 he was witnessing the ritual and commenting on it and Zechariah alike. We've already heard how important living water was to Jesus, since he'd discoursed about it at length with the Samaritan woman, even though she and her kind refused to make the pilgrimage to Mount Zion in Jerusalem at Sukkot, or at any other time, for that matter.

But Jesus announces that he can give living water to anyone, any-where. So he declares on the eighth day, "If anyone thirsts, let him come to me and drink. Whoever believes in me, as the Scripture has said, 'Out of his heart will flow rivers of living water'" (7:38).

A scribe might ask, in all fairness, *where* exactly does the Scripture say this?

The closest you can get is Proverbs 18:4, "The words of a man's mouth are deep waters; the fountain of wisdom is a bubbling brook," but that hardly seems adequate to the stakes of Jesus' declaration. Song of Songs alludes to a "well of living water" (4:15), though in a *very* different context.

More likely Jesus was modifying Zechariah's association of Jerusalem with living waters to make it clear that God himself is their source. Jeremiah had already made that move. The prophet levels, in God's voice, the accusation that "my people have committed two evils: they have forsaken me, the fountain of living waters, and hewed out cisterns for themselves, broken cisterns that can hold no water" (2:13). Later Jeremiah prophesies, "O LORD, the hope of Israel, all who forsake you shall be put to shame; those who turn away from you shall be written in the earth, for they have forsaken the LORD, the fountain of living water" (17:13).

The Book of Revelation will eventually turn these negatives into a positive with its own prophecy: "For the Lamb in the midst of the throne will be their shepherd, and he will guide them to springs of living water, and God will wipe away every tear from their eyes" (7:17).

John the Evangelist, however, is less concerned with citing his source and more concerned with *what* exactly Jesus is talking about. Those living waters are, in fact, "the Spirit, whom those who believed in him were to receive, for as yet the Spirit had not been given, be-cause Jesus was not yet glorified" (7:39). Note the linkage of both Sukkot and the Spirit to the glory of Jesus! The apostle Paul would approve.

But whereas the Synoptic Transfiguration confirmed the disci-ples' rejection of false hypotheses about Jesus' identity in favor of the correct confession, the outcome of the Festival of Tabernacles in John is to sow further confusion among the crowds. *Now* they start saying Jesus is "the prophet." When others suppose he's the Christ, immediately they are contradicted: "Is the Christ to come from Galilee? Has not the Scripture said that the Christ comes from the offspring of David, and comes from Bethlehem, the village where David was?" (7:42).

Despite this, John confirms what Zechariah announced, namely that the true and right celebration of Sukkot will be an eschatological event of universal significance. Zechariah foresaw the following postscript to the horrors: "Then everyone who survives of all the nations that have come against Jerusalem shall go up year after year to worship the King, the LORD of hosts, and to keep the Feast of Booths. And if any of the families of the earth do not go up to Jerusalem to worship the King, the LORD of hosts, there will be no rain on them. And if the family of Egypt does not go up and present themselves, then on them there shall be no rain; there shall be the plague with which the LORD afflicts the nations that do not go up to keep the Feast of Booths. This shall be the punishment to Egypt and the punishment to all the nations that do not go up to keep the Feast of Booths" (14:16–19).

Still not the most cheerful of prophecies. But an improvement on what's come so far.

Anyway, if the point is to receive the blessings of the harvest gathered in, why *wouldn't* you want to join the merrymaking? Why choose drought when you could have welcome rain and rivers of living water?

Even this is only drawing out the predicates of the premise stated at the outset. John told you all you needed to know about Jesus and the eschatological Sukkot right back in his first chapter, in his opening soliloquy. "And the word became flesh and tabernacled [*eskḗnōsen*] among us, and we beheld his glory, the glory as of the only-begotten of the Father, full of grace and truth" (1:14).[19]

It's our old friend *skēnḗ*, embedded in a verb form, evoking all the possibilities of the Septuagint's translation of the Hebrew: a tent, a booth, and a tabernacle all in one. The Word puts on our rugged and temporary flesh in order to be God in our midst and gather for himself an eschatological harvest.

The Gospel of John's third-cousin-once-removed, the Book of Revelation, makes an *inclusio* of its own, the end contained in the beginning: "And I heard a big voice from the throne saying, Behold, the tabernacle of God is among people, and he will tabernacle with them, and they will be his people, and he will be their God" (21:3).[20]

But will God indeed dwell on the earth?

27 But I say to you all truly,
there are certain of those standing here
who will no way, no how taste death
until they should have seen
the kingdom of God.

28 And it came to be
about eight days
after these sayings
and taking along
Peter and John and James
he ascended the mountain
to pray.

29 And in his praying
the appearance of his face
came to be different
and his clothing
lightning-white.

30 And behold
two men
were talking together to him,
these same were
Moses and Elijah,

31 who appearing in glory
were speaking of his exodus
which he was about to fulfill
in Jerusalem.

32 But Peter
and those with him
were being weighed down with sleep;

but waking up they saw
his glory

and the two men
standing together with him.

33 And it came to be
in their departing from him
Peter said to Jesus,

Master,
it is good for us to be here,
and how about I make
three tabernacles,
one for you and
one for Moses and
one for Elijah,

not seeing what he says.

34 But him saying these things,
a cloud came to be
and overshadowed them;

but they were frightened
in their entering into the cloud.

35 And a voice came to be
from the cloud
saying,

This is my Son,
the one who has been chosen;
listen to him.

36 And in the coming to be of the voice
Jesus was found alone.

And they kept silent
and announced to nobody in those days
anything that they had seen.

Eyewitnesses : Peter, James, and John

Years later, Peter still reached for tabernacles when he had something to say.

In the opening chapter of his Second Epistle, he urges his readers to remain steadfast in the faith, because he won't be with them much longer to hold their steadfastness steady. And who knows better than Peter how quickly steadfastness can vanish?

"I consider it right," he tells us, "as long as I am in this tabernacle, to awake you in remembrance, perceiving as I do that the laying-aside of my tabernacle is soon, just as also our Lord Jesus Christ declared to me. And I will be diligent that, after my exodus, you may always be able to make remembrance of these things" (1:13–14).[21] Like Jesus, Peter calls his imminent death an exodus. Like Paul, Peter calls his body a tabernacle.

Who knows? It may have been the use of those very terms that turned Peter's mind toward the Transfiguration—complete with his infamously inept proposal to build three tabernacles for the august personages assembled on the mountaintop—for, just a few verses later, he recalls and recounts the event.

That, at least, would make good sense of the text as it stands. Yet if there is one single thing New Testament scholars agree on, it's that the First and Second Epistles of Peter were most definitely *not* composed by the same author. Leave out the names, and you'd never otherwise think to associate the two letters with each other. They differ widely in vocabulary, style, setting, and theological preoccupations.

Whether either was written by Peter is another matter. I incline to the view, shared by some scholars, that what we call First Peter is the result of Paul's scribe Silas (also known as Silvanus) writing down an oral dictation by Peter, as the closing verses of the Epistle report and internal evidence may support, albeit inconclusively.

But if that's the case, with the textual and stylistic evidence overwhelmingly refuting the same author behind both Epistles, then Peter simply *cannot* have written the Second Epistle attributed to him.

Which is not to suggest that Second Peter is therefore worthless; not at all. Apostolicity in the early church was a criterion of content, not presumed authorship, which is why the unsigned Epistle to the Hebrews made it into the canon, while writings under venerable apostolic names, such as the Gospel of James or the Acts of Paul, failed to make the cut.

What makes the Second Epistle of Peter's likely pseudonymity awkward, though, is not just the name under which it claims to be written. The issue is the not-Peter author appealing to an episode in real-Peter's life, to the point of saying that he and his companions were "eyewitnesses" (1:16, *epóptai*—note the root of our word "optics," same as in Synoptic).

That episode is, of course, the Transfiguration. Second Peter contains the only unambiguous reference to the event of the Transfiguration in the New Testament outside of the Synoptic Gospels—though it neither uses the term "transfigured" like Mark and Matthew do, nor does it describe the change that overcomes Jesus apart from generic references to splendor, honor, and glory.

Still. The reference to the Transfiguration is undoubtedly what confirmed its veracity as Peter's own writing and commended its inclusion in what would eventually become the New Testament canon.

We shouldn't let contemporary standards of authorship and attribution cloud the issue, even in a story that prominently features a cloud! Assuming Second Peter isn't the handwritten work of the original disciple by that name, it nevertheless stands in some kind of relationship to him, whether as a memory from Peter passed down in the congregations that knew him, or as an appeal to his unique experience and unrivaled authority. If the former, Second Peter may be an independent attestation of the Transfiguration; if the latter, it's the fruit of further reflection and discernment on the event in the early decades of the church.[22]

Such are our problems with Second Peter today. But in the early church, not only was Peter's authorship not in question; neither was the Transfiguration itself. If anything, what is extraordinary about

Second Peter's witness is that, out of all possible events in the life of Christ, it selects the Transfiguration as the guarantee of its message! Not his angel-announced conception or his Resurrection appearances to more than five hundred at a time; not his Baptism with the visible descent of the Spirit or his feeding of the five thousand.

Instead, this Epistle's public proof is one of the most private events in Jesus' life, attested by only three eyewitnesses.

Why this event? And why these witnesses?

We'll have to call on the Synoptics for help.

With the Transfiguration situated at the dead center of Mark's Gospel, what leads up to it is crucial for its interpretation.

In the chapter preceding, the Pharisees demand a sign. Jesus refuses. He goes on to heal the blind man at Bethsaida. It's a strange healing story, since the first try doesn't quite work. The half-healed man thinks people look like "trees, walking" (8:24), as if Shakespeare's "Macbeth" jumped backwards in time a millennium and a half before returning to Jacobean England where it belongs.

Then we come to the real preface to the Transfiguration. Jesus and his disciples are way up north in the villages of Caesarea Philippi, and as they're ambling along Jesus asks, you can imagine almost casually, "So what are the people saying about me? Who do folks think I am?"

The reported rumors pick out John the Baptist, presumably recapitulated, or Elijah, presumably having returned on a fiery chariot the same way he departed, or just any old prophet—pick your favorite. Jesus appears unsurprised by the general misapprehension.

But for once he expects a lot of his disciples. "Uh-huh; and who do *you* think I am?" And for once, they deliver.

Peter, bright and shiny, raises his hand and pronounces his lesson like an A+ student: "You're the Christ! 'Messiah' if we're using Hebrew in class today. The anointed one! The expected one! The eschatological wunderkind who will usher in a neverending Sukkot of merrymaking!" If Peter doesn't say it quite so plainly, evidently he thinks it.

Yet the moment Jesus accepts and acknowledges this title, he swears them to secrecy and proceeds to unfold a plan that looks nothing like Sukkot and everything like Passover, especially if the starring role goes to neither Moses nor Pharaoh but to the sacrificial lamb. The firstborn Son of Man must suffer, must be rejected, must be killed. Of course, afterwards, he will rise again, but the disciples appear not to hear a word of that part—and later, even when they do, they appear not to understand a word of that part.

Peter is so crushingly embarrassed for his teacher—for how can even the best of pupils exceed his teacher? It's a horrifying moment for a hero-worshipper like Peter—that he has to pull Jesus aside, talk him off the ledge, put a stop to this defeatist talk, nudge him toward a better reading of the Scriptures.

What happens next rivals Peter's infamous denial for the worst moment of his life. At least in the latter episode, Jesus utters no accusation and is proven to have been right all along. Cold comfort, but it's something. In *this* moment, the teacher not only breaks free from the private consultation to return to the other, lesser pupils; not only rebukes his star student and accuses him of failing to learn his lessons, however perfect his grades may be; but actually calls him by the worst name, the name of the ultimate enemy, as if Peter's devotion were in fact possession.

And why? Because between Peter's confession of the Christ and Peter proving himself a lackey of Satan stands the cross.

After this dreadful confrontation Jesus draws the inner circle out, summons the crowd, and disseminates a version of the same story for public consumption. "If anyone would come after me, let him deny himself and take up his cross and follow me" (8:34). Little do they know how literally Jesus means what he says! Life is at stake in losing it, so is keeping your soul, and in the end what else is there of you but your soul? If you lose your soul, how can there even be a *you* left to possess anything, should it be the whole world?

It all comes down to what you're ashamed of: either of Jesus, or of denying Jesus. It's a lesson Peter will have to learn again and again and again.

Matthew more or less follows Mark's lead. His Pharisees keep unusual company with the Sadducees, their temporary bond forged over a mutual dislike of Jesus.

When Peter confesses the Christ, Matthew expands Jesus' response to, "Blessed are you, Simon Bar-Jonah! For flesh and blood has not revealed this to you, but my Father who is in heaven" (16:17)—better accounting for Peter's failure immediately thereafter: only a revelation from above could explain how Peter managed to get it right when he usually gets it wrong. Upping the stakes even more, here Matthew alone of the Evangelists awards Peter the title of foundation rock of the church, a pun on his nickname *pétros*, which means "rock." These distinctive blessings upon Peter make even starker Jesus' pivot to calling him Satan.

Luke prefaces the Transfiguration rather differently. Jesus sends the twelve disciples out on their first preaching mission, during which time Herod suffers a great deal of perplexity as he guesses incorrectly at the identity of Jesus. On the disciples' return, Jesus sets about feeding the five thousand. The main point of overlap with Mark is that this happens in the vicinity of Bethsaida, where Mark's Jesus healed the blind man. Thereafter Luke converges with his Synoptic fellows.

All three Gospels agree on the transition point. They link the question about Jesus' identity to the Transfiguration by way of Jesus' prophecy that certain ones standing there would no way, no how taste death before seeing the kingdom of God come in power.

Certain *ones*, not *a* certain *one*. It's time to give Peter a chance to flee the limelight and lick his wounds, while the two other eyewitnesses endure our closer inspection.

James and John are favorites of Mark's, nearly as much as Peter. They always appear as a pair, which might seem inevitable since they're brothers, sons of Zebedee. Yet Peter's own brother, Andrew, flits in and out of the scene, anything but an inevitable companion for Peter.

Anyway, biblical brothers are not always so fond of each other. James and John seem to be a rare case of brothers who'd rather be together than apart. Jesus gave them a nickname, *Boanerges*, "Sons of Thunder" (Mark 3:17, omitted in Matthew and Luke). That already puts them in good company with Peter—originally Simon—as the only disciples to receive nicknames from the Lord.

James and John make their first appearance just after Jesus calls Peter and Andrew. While those two left their boats behind, James and John leave their father behind. At least Zebedee has servants to pick up his sons' slack. Luke modifies the story slightly: James and John are Peter's partners, and Peter's brother Andrew turns up only later.

After Jesus' first sermon and exorcism in the synagogue, both pairs of brothers follow Jesus into Peter and Andrew's house, there to witness his healing of Peter's mother-in-law, followed by a flood of the afflicted.

The first time Peter, James, and John are picked out as a special trio is in the interwoven tale of the woman with the issue of blood and Jairus' daughter. By the time they reach the house, news comes that the girl is dead. Commanding the grieving father not to fear but only believe, Jesus selects to come with him "Peter and James and John the brother of James"—a curious designation, since there are two Jameses but only one John (Mark 3:17–18). Shouldn't it be James the brother of John to distinguish him from James the son of Alphaeus? Or so a little brother would presumably argue to his big brother.

In any case, this invitation makes Peter, James, and John the sole eyewitnesses to a healing that might just be a resurrection from the dead. Or if not a resurrection in the unique and baffling sense of Jesus' Resurrection, then certainly a rescue from the jaws of Sheol. It functions, in some way, as a preparation or initiation to qualify as witnesses to the Transfiguration, which is the next time this threesome will be set apart from the others.

Yet while Peter, when he fails, fails immediately and spectacularly—what with his attempt to instruct Jesus to give up this cross business, and his stuttering suggestion of tabernacles—James and John fail slowly and humiliatingly. Peter's errors spring from misplaced love. James and John's, from pride. They covet prestige. When *they* set their minds on things of man rather than of God, it's to scheme and maneuver toward the acquisition of glory. Their own.

Not too long after the Transfiguration, Jesus delivers his third

Passion prediction. It's more detailed than the first two: "See, we are going up to Jerusalem, and the Son of Man will be delivered over to the chief priests and the scribes, and they will condemn him to death and deliver him over to the Gentiles. And they will mock him and spit on him, and flog him and kill him. And after three days he will rise" (Mark 10:33–34).

At exactly this point, the sons of Zebedee intervene to demonstrate how well they've learned their lessons. Peter isn't the only A student in this class! "Teacher, we're gonna ask you something, and you have to do it, before we even tell you what it is. Are you game?"

Never mind that the last time such an offer was made and accepted, it involved John the Baptist's head. Or the immense quantity of ancient literature, both biblical and pagan, spelling out the always-disastrous results of a rash vow. Jesus wisely replies, "How about you tell me what you have in mind first?"

The idea spills out. You get the impression the brothers are immensely pleased to have come up with a proposal that equalizes the two of them. The fact that their equalization with each other exalts them above all the other disciples escapes their notice.

It doesn't, of course, escape the notice of the other ten—but only after they find out it's a bad idea. You can tell they weren't quite sure of that, or their right to be indignant about it, until Jesus confirms it.

Instead of playing the game, Jesus states the plain truth: "You do not know what you are asking. Are you able to drink the cup that I drink, or to be baptized with the baptism with which I am baptized?" (10:38). Notably, this is the first use of baptism in this Gospel as a metaphor for death—a subtle kinship to Romans 6.

Either James and John still miss the point, or they're too stubborn to back down. Pride answers: "We *are* able!"

Jesus agrees that a baptism is coming for them, without affirming that it will be due to their own ability. But he disavows any right to grant their request about the seating arrangements of heaven.

More importantly, Jesus denies their right to want what they want. "Whoever would be first among you must be slave of all. For even the Son of Man came not to *be* served but *to* serve, and to give his life as a ransom for many" (10:44–45).

The brothers' prideful request is turned back to Jesus' own purposes: preparing them, and the other disciples, for suffering and death.

Matthew is so embarrassed by this episode he shifts the blame onto their mother—then apologizes to Mrs. Zebedee by allowing her to be one of the witnesses of the risen Jesus.

Luke deletes the episode altogether, but he has his own way of demonstrating the Zebedee boys' failure to grasp the point. Not long after the Transfiguration, Luke following Mark reports how John tattled that "we saw someone casting out demons in your name, and we tried to stop him, because he was not following us" (Mark 9:38, Luke 9:49). Jesus tells him to stop telling them to stop.

Then Luke adds a story unique to him, maybe because of his unique interest in the Samaritans. Jesus now knows that the days are drawing near for him to be taken up, so he sets his face toward Jerusalem and sends messengers ahead to make preparations for him in a Samaritan village. But because of his destination in the rival pilgrimage city of Jerusalem, the Samaritans reject him.

James and John are united in their outrage on the teacher's behalf. "Lord, do you want us to tell fire to come down from heaven and consume them?" (Luke 9:54). Pride desires to wreak its destruction once again. For the moment Jesus simply rebukes them into silence. In the next chapter, he pointedly makes the hero of his most famous parable a Samaritan.

Some years on, Jesus' complete rejoinder to the fire-and-brimstone brothers will arrive with the faith and baptism of many Samaritans in response to Philip's preaching. Peter and John son of Zebedee will be sent by the Jerusalem church to Samaria to investigate the unauthorized extension of baptism to these marginal members of Israel.

Luke has prepared us for this specific Peter-John pairing, without James. In his version of the Transfiguration, the eyewitnesses are listed as "Peter, John, and James" (9:28)—inverting the order of the last two as recorded in Mark and Matthew. Luke also informs us that Jesus sent Peter and John only to prepare the Passover supper.

Anyway, once Peter and John get to Samaria, they're convinced by the faith they find and lay hands on the Samaritans, who thereby receive the Holy Spirit. And so at last, the fire does indeed come down upon the Samaritans, just as the sons of Zebedee always wanted.

But not at all in the way they expected.

Back to Mark. In the final lead-up to the Crucifixion, both pairs of brothers approach Jesus—not only James and John, but Peter and Andrew as well—to ask the teacher privately about signs of the temple's imminent destruction (13:3–4). They get a lot more than they bargained for, about not just the end of the temple but the end of all things.

Maybe Andrew didn't handle the news well. He drops out of the action again when Jesus takes Peter, James, and John to the Garden of Gethsemane to pray. Just as well for Andrew. He didn't have to suffer the shame of falling asleep while Jesus prays in sorrow and anguish. Peter of course reappears in the drama to unfold, but this is the last we hear of James and John in Mark's Gospel.

Curiously enough, only the Gospel of John numbers the sons of Zebedee among the witnesses to the Resurrection (21:2).

While the exact configuration of Peter, James, and John never re-appears after the Gospels, we do learn bits and pieces more about them in their new apostolic vocation.[23] They are named in sequence, Andrew once again appended, in the company of disciples praying in the upper room between the Ascension and Pentecost (Acts 1:13). Peter dominates the first half of Acts, all the way up to the faith and baptism of Cornelius and his Gentile household (chs. 10, 11, and 15), but in his early ministry among the Jews, John son of Zebedee is Peter's closest companion (chs. 3 and 4).

James son of Zebedee is mentioned only one more time, when he meets a martyr's end. "About that time Herod the king laid vio-lent hands on some who belonged to the church. He killed James the brother of John with the sword, and when he saw that it pleased the Jews, he proceeded to arrest Peter also" (Acts 12:1–3).

While Second Peter doesn't mention James and John by name, the choice of pronoun does notably shift from "I" in the first fifteen introductory verses to "we" in the account of the Transfiguration: "We made known to you all... And we heard this voice having been borne from heaven" (1:16, 18), the second "we" being spelled out in the text, despite being grammatically unnecessary. Whatever the connection to the real Peter, the account in this Epistle carefully preserves the fact that Peter had company on this most extraordinary of occasions.

When Peter, James, and John appear together, it's always and only because Jesus selected them. So it is at the Transfiguration. "Jesus takes along Peter and James and John, and he bears them up to a high mountain by themselves alone" (Mark 9:2), a double verb stressing Jesus' initiative and choice.

Peter gets chosen, no doubt, for his confession of Jesus as the Christ. But oddly enough, that title has no place in the Transfiguration story itself. Nor do the Synoptics agree on the alternative honorific that Peter supplies—only that, somehow, he can't bring himself to say "Christ." Maybe the unnerving talk of the cross sowed doubts in Peter's mind.

According to Mark, Peter's proposal of tabernacles is prefaced by "Rabbi," which means more to us now than it probably did then. It wouldn't necessarily have signified a religious teacher per se, though it was a title of honor, something like "my lord" (without the connotation of the LORD) or "my great one." Peter invokes the term again in his wonderment at the withered fig tree; blind Bartimaeus uses it interchangeably with "Son of David"; and ominously enough, it's what Judas calls out right before planting that treacherous kiss.

Matthew seems to have nothing but negative associations with "Rabbi." In his Gospel only Judas addresses Jesus this way, of course at the betrayal but also earlier, at the Last Supper, when inquiring whether Jesus knew what he was about to do. Matthew's Jesus twice warns against those who covet the title.

So at the Transfiguration, Matthew has Peter say "Lord" (kýrie), an honorific that appears all over his Gospel and switches freely from referring to the Lord God of Israel to Jesus himself, the slippage intentional in a way that Mark only rarely allows.

Luke loves "Lord" even more than Matthew, but he changes

Peter's term yet again to "Master," in Greek *epistáta*. The term means literally one who stands-over and is used only by Luke and only in his Gospel. Peter speaks it three times in all; John son of Zebedee once; all the disciples twice in succession when their boat is sinking; and, the last time, when ten lepers plead for healing.

If any common thread can be found connecting all these uses of *epistáta*, it might be that of people who call on Jesus because they recognize his power, yet without the slightest notion of who they're really dealing with.

Not only do the Evangelists differ on what Peter called Jesus; they also differ on what motivated him to speak in the first place.

In Mark, it's fear. Fear is threaded throughout this Gospel. It's something that must first be learned. The disciples don't know Jesus well enough to fear him until he stills the storm. Then for the first time they fear, murmuring, "Who *is* this man? Even the wind and the sea obey his word!" (4:41). The verb here, which reappears in various forms, is *ephobéthēsan*, with the root *phob-*, whence of course English "phobia."

Once you know Jesus well enough to fear him, he teaches you *not* to fear him. He does this, the first time, right before raising Jairus's daughter. "Fear not, only believe" (5:36). And again, when he walks on water: "It is I. Fear not" (6:50). What has to be expressed in English as "It is I" is in literal Greek "I am," as in the first part of God's holy name. "*I AM.* Fear not." Mark's Jesus will deploy *I AM* again when he is on trial before the council. John's Jesus will deploy *I AM* extensively, culminating in the moment of his arrest when the very utterance of these syllables knocks his pursuers to the ground.

The Transfiguration, of all events, marks the high point—literally and figuratively—of the disciples' fear. They are not just scared in the usual way, as they will continue to be on many occasions thereafter. On the mountaintop, they are *ékphoboi* (9:6), an adjective that appends the prefix *ek-* to the root, intensifying it to something like "scared *out of* their wits." Or we might extrapolate permission to pun from Jesus and say that Peter was *petrified*.

According to Mark, it's Jesus' gleaming white clothes, plus the apparition of Elijah and Moses, that deprive Peter, James, and John of their wits. It is *not* the voice from the cloud that does it. This is where Matthew diverges. His trio remains calm and collected through the light show, even the metamorphosis of Jesus' very face. Fear doesn't strike them until after the voice declares Jesus to be his beloved Son. So these two Evangelists agree on the fear reaction, only not precisely what the fear is in response to. And Matthew's fear is somewhat less fearful than Mark's.

Mark returns to ordinary fear after the fact. After they've come down the mountain, after the healing of the boy with the unclean spirit, Jesus teaches again about his death and Resurrection. "But they did not understand the saying, and were afraid to ask him" (9:32). Not the kind of afraid that makes you babble incoherently. But enough to make you want to avoid the topic and argue instead about which of you is the greatest.

If fear-out-of-your-wits characterizes the centerpiece of Mark's Gospel, then it is no surprise that fear concludes his Gospel as well. Famously, the last words of the oldest manuscripts are the inconclusive, "for they feared" (16:8). It's even stranger than it sounds in English. The Greek is *ephoboûnto gár*, that *gár* being a postpositive conjunction, meaning it can't stand in the first place in a clause. But it's pretty weird to stand in the last place, not just in a sentence but in an entire written work! It leaves you suspended in the fear that the women felt at the announcement of Jesus' Resurrection.

And yet, they must have told somebody, sometime. How else would you even know that they'd ever been afraid? Matthew, Luke, and John all find other and rather more appealing literary devices to signal that, even though the narrative of Jesus' life, death, and Resurrection has ended, the story is most definitely not over. But Mark takes no prisoners and offers no concessions. Who *is* this that wind and sea obey him, Elijah and Moses respond to his summons, and he gains life by way of shameful death?

Luke, for his part, knows a thing or two about fear. The word comes up six times in his first chapter alone. But he shifts the locus of fear in the Transfiguration scene once again. It's neither the sight of Jesus and his companions nor the voice from heaven that unglues the disciples, but the cloud, or more specifically, "their entering into the cloud" (9:34).

More surprising is that Luke proposes a different driving force behind the disciples' reactions: sleepiness.

It seems underwhelming. Peter, James, and John have just hiked up a mountain, so maybe they were honestly tired out. Luke is vague on when exactly the disciples started being weighed down with sleep, but it could be they missed the onset of the change to Jesus and the sudden appearance of Moses and Elijah, not to mention the content of their conversation. They wake up and see what's going on: glory, without context or explanation. Luke has Moses and Elijah departing at the very moment the disciples wake up, so Peter, realizing all the fun he's missed, barks out the first thing that comes to his groggy mind. Luke in kindly fashion describes it as "not seeing what he says" (9:33), unlike Mark's attribution to fear and Matthew's polite refusal to pass judgment at all.

Probably Luke is either borrowing from or foreshadowing the Garden of Gethsemane. All three Synoptics agree on the same three disciples' failure to stay awake and pray on this last night of Jesus' life. The master is saddened but hardly surprised by their being overcome by sleep. After all, they'd done it before.

It could also be that all three Synoptics are alluding to a still earlier precedent for human mishandling of divine self-disclosure.

When the prophet Daniel received visions, two reactions overtook him: fear and sleep. "When I, Daniel, had seen the vision, I sought to understand it. And behold, there stood before me one having the appearance of a man. And I heard a man's voice between the banks of the Ulai, and it called, 'Gabriel, make this man understand the vision.' So he came near where I stood. And when he came, I was *frightened* and fell on my face. But he said to me, 'Understand, O son of man, that the vision is for the time of the end.' And when he had spoken to me, I fell into a *deep sleep* with my face to the ground. But he touched me and made me stand up" (8:15–18). Fear and sleep characterize a second divine apparition in Daniel 10:7–9.

All three Synoptics borrow fear from Daniel, Luke alone borrows sleep, and Matthew borrows something else: vision. Matthew's Jesus alone names what has happened. "Tell the vision [*hórama*] to not one single person until when the Son of Man is raised from the dead" (17:9). The term might mislead readers today, connoting something imagined or hallucinated, rather than something that actually happened. Matthew doesn't mean it that way, not least of all because the focus of the vision, Jesus himself, is still with the disciples after the fact.

The word is a one-off in Matthew's Gospel. Curiously enough, though Luke never uses it in his own Gospel, it's a key term in Acts. Assuming a common intention, the occurrences of *hórama* in Acts show us that visions are real communications of the real God, just outside the usual channels. Hence Stephen's characterization of Moses beholding the burning bush, the mutual visions of Saul and Ananias, Peter's vision preparing him for the faith of Cornelius the Gentile as well as something he *mistook* for a vision but was actually an angel liberating him from prison, the Macedonians summoning Paul to help them, and the Lord promising to protect Paul as he continues to preach despite the hostile reception to his message.

Then again, what good is a vision?

After all, anyone can claim to have had a vision. A vision's unique and narrow scope gives it both its potency *and* its implausibility.

On the other hand, if implausibility is an issue, then the real problem with the Transfiguration is its sheer unimpressiveness.

Ovid, a Roman contemporary of Jesus', could fill twelve thousand lines of verse with metamorphoses, from Jupiter becoming a ram and Juno a snow-white cow to the pious elderly couple Baucis and Philemon escaping grief by being transformed into intertwining oak and linden trees. Ovid describes metamorphoses to explain the origins of everything from the lapwing, bullfinch, ibis, crow, owl, and hawk to the Rhodope mountain range—mostly the result of divine mischief, human uppityness, or both.

Whereas all Mark can manage is a gleaming white tunic, Matthew and Luke barely more.

The Transfiguration is anything but a sophisticated myth (*sesoph-*

isménois mýthois), the fabrication of sophists, as Second Peter points out. A sophisticated myth would make grander claims with longer-lasting effects. It would *explain* things.

But the Transfiguration raises far more questions than it answers, including the question the disciples walk away with: "disputing what it is, to rise from the dead" (Mark 9:10). It's still not clear why, out of all possible events, the author of Second Peter insists on the Transfiguration to make his case.

But maybe that's because we aren't yet clear enough on what case, exactly, Second Peter is making.

Splendor and majestic glory seem like obvious signs after the fact, but at the Transfiguration itself the bright light left the eyewitnesses in the dark. For the dazzling clothing was the sign, but the obscuring cloud was the source.

It is time to move into the cloud.

Or rather: the time has come for the cloud to overshadow us.

Cloud : God the Father

The Transfiguration story begins and ends with being alone. Jesus bears the three disciples alone of the dozen up to the mountaintop. When it's all over, Jesus alone is left with them.

Aloneness is not in fact very alone. To be singled out is not to be lonely.

Even in the middle of the lonely place on the mountaintop, the four are not alone. The elite of Israel's history turn up in the personages of Moses and Elijah. Maybe Peter's mistake was, as much as anything, to be satisfied too soon. For one is coming, one who is quite possibly always there, present if not seen, ubiquitous yet hidden, near and aloof at once, akin to the master or the king in so many of Jesus' parables. Like water that evaporates invisibly into the sky and takes visible form high above before dropping down again as rain, so this present invisibility, this ubiquitous hiddenness, comes to the senses in the form of a cloud.

Clouds and this Presence are old friends. They coincide across the Scriptures of Israel. But foundational for all their co-incidences is their co-incidence in Exodus. If Moses wasn't enough to alert Peter that he was in a Passover story, if the term *exodus* wasn't enough to do it, then the cloud should have taken away any lingering doubts.

Because *how* the cloud makes its appearance in Exodus matters, too. Not just for clarifying what story we're in, but clarifying what God we're dealing with.

The long preamble with Moses's prehistory is over. So are the first skirmishes with Pharaoh. We've had nine plagues, each worse than the last. One hard heart remains immovably hard. God threatens a tenth plague.

All the other plagues are incidental, in a sense. They are specific to the time and place—the kind of plagues that would really get to agricultural Egyptians dependent on the Nile. You could substitute one plague for another if the story were happening at the Arctic Circle or on a Pacific island and still get the same idea. You could also explain the first nine plagues naturalistically, if you wanted to.

But the tenth plague has a long reach. The curse is not natural or circumstantial but metaphysical. It inscribes creation itself with trenches so deep that only the blood of God will fill them. So let us track carefully the unfolding sequence of events and information.

In Exodus 11, God threatens the death of the firstborn. In chapter 12, the Israelites are given and undertake their Passover preparations to spare the lives of their firstborn males. Then the plague strikes and every Egyptian house is turned into a house of mourning, at which exact point the Israelites make a run for it.

But all the action stops right here, suspended between death and freedom. The instructions regarding the Passover are repeated, even as the crumbs still sit on the table. God makes a claim that looms almost as threateningly as the plague itself. "Consecrate to me all the firstborn. Whatever is the first to open the womb among the people of Israel, both of man and of beast, is mine" (13:2). *Mine*—for what purpose?

Moses speaks up now to repeat for a third time instructions regarding the festival, this time stressing the unleavened bread over the sacrificial lamb. But even unleavened bread still leads directly into the same strong divine claim. "You shall set apart to the LORD all that first opens the womb. All the firstborn of your animals that are males shall be the LORD's" (13:12), in memory of the tenth plague that took the Egyptians' firstborn males.

The uncanny truth behind the plague is that its fatal action is universal and undiscriminating. The only difference is that Israel has been given the key of redemption to seize their baby boys back from God's hand. Therefore they are to testify: "I sacrifice to the LORD all the males that first open the womb, but all the firstborn of my sons I redeem" (13:15).

Immediately after that, the cloud makes its first appearance.

We are back in the action now. The people are running for their lives, Joseph's bones in tow. Despite this, the temptation to return to bondage is so overwhelming that both God and Moses have to get tactical. They don't take the fastest route, in case the Israelites run into Philistines and get spooked. They head for the wilderness instead. "And the LORD went before them by day in a pillar of cloud to lead them along the way, and by night in a pillar of fire to give them light, that they might travel by day and by night. The pillar of cloud by day and the pillar of fire by night did not depart from before the people" (13:21–22).

When Pharaoh changes his mind—again—and decides to pursue the runaways, the cloud places itself between him and them. Moses promises, "The LORD will fight for you, and you have only to be silent" (14:14). After leading Israel through the parted sea, "the LORD in the pillar of fire and of cloud looked down on the Egyptian forces and threw the Egyptian forces into a panic" (14:24). That is the end of their pursuit.

But the cloud does not depart. It stays on and manifests the Lord's glory to feed the grumbling Israelites with manna and quail. When they reach Mount Sinai, and the Lord proposes a new covenant that the people in turn accept, the cloud is its visible confirmation: "Behold, I am coming to you in a thick cloud, that the people may hear when I speak with you, and may also believe you forever" (19:9). Then, "on the morning of the third day there were thunders and lightnings and a thick cloud on the mountain and a very loud trumpet blast, so that all the people in the camp trembled" (19:16–20).

The details of the covenant follow: the Ten Commandments; regulations concerning altars, slaves, and restitution; the Sabbath and the three major festivals; the promised land. The covenant is ratified by Moses and his three companions, together with the elders. The shed blood of sacrifice is thrown against both altar and people: "Behold the blood of the covenant that the LORD has made with you in accordance with all these words" (24:8).

When Moses returns to the mountain alone, "the cloud covered the mountain. The glory of the LORD dwelt on Mount Sinai, and the cloud covered it six days. And on the seventh day he called to Moses out of the midst of the cloud. Now the appearance of the glory of the LORD was like a devouring fire on the top of the mountain in the sight of the people of Israel. Moses entered the cloud and went up on the mountain. And Moses was on the mountain forty days and forty nights" (24:15–18). More laws follow, specifically with regard to the ark of the covenant and the furnishings of the tabernacle, and the craftsmen who will make all these things.

All is going very well. So, of course, the people demand a golden calf to worship.

God in response announces it's time to leave Sinai, but he'll stay behind, "lest I consume you on the way" (33:3). Moses realizes he has to do something to mediate between God and the people. Neither dares draw near to the other, for rather different reasons. So the tabernacle comes to serve a dual purpose as the traveling miniature of Mount Sinai.

As with Sinai, so with the tabernacle—the people keep their distance. Moses concedes it's better that way. "Moses used to take the tent [*ohel*] and pitch it outside the camp, far off from the camp, and he called it the tent of meeting. And everyone who sought the LORD would go out to the tent of meeting, which was outside the camp. Whenever Moses went out to the tent, all the people would rise up, and each would stand at his tent door, and watch Moses until he had gone into the tent. When Moses entered the tent, the pillar of cloud would descend and stand at the entrance of the tent, and the LORD would speak with Moses. And when all the people saw the pillar of cloud standing at the entrance of the tent, all the people would rise up and worship, each at his tent door. Thus the LORD used to speak to Moses face to face, as a man speaks to his friend" (33:7–11; cf. Leviticus 16:2, Deuteronomy 31:15).

On the basis of this new arrangement with Moses as mediator, God relents: "My presence will go with you, and I will give you rest" (33:14). Moses decides then and there to push his luck: "Please show me your glory" (33:18). God partially agrees.

After Moses cuts two new tablets of stone to receive the law again, he ascends Mount Sinai into the cloud once more. "The LORD descended in the cloud and stood with him there, and proclaimed the name of the LORD. The LORD passed before him and proclaimed, 'The LORD, the LORD, a God merciful and gracious, slow to anger, and abounding in steadfast love and faithfulness, keeping steadfast love for thousands, forgiving iniquity and transgression and sin, but who will by no means clear the guilty, visiting the iniquity of the fathers on the children and the children's children, to the third and the fourth generation'" (34:5–7, cf. 33:19–23).

Recall the sequence here: God's claim on firstborn males and sparing of firstborn males and *not* sparing of firstborn males, followed by the cloud, the covenant, the glory, and the blood. And now, *the name.*

In the decision to spare Israel in the wilderness, God names himself afresh, still the Lord, but now more specifically the Lord who is merciful and gracious, abounding in steadfast love. The name comes forth from the cloud that is the earthly location of God's heavenly glory.

Moses, in reply, asks of God three things. Go in our midst. Pardon our sin. Take us for your inheritance.

The Lord renews the covenant again, promulgates the law again, commands the three festivals while claiming the firstborn males again and requiring "all your males" to appear "before the LORD God, the God of Israel" (34:23).

At precisely this point, Moses is transfigured. "When Moses came down from Mount Sinai, with the two tablets of the testimony in his hand as he came down from the mountain, Moses did not know that the skin of his face shone because he had been talking with God. Aaron and all the people of Israel saw Moses, and behold, the skin of his face shone, and they were afraid to come near him" (34:29–30).

Yet for all Moses's close friendship with God, despite his transfiguration, a limit remains. He never sees God's full glory. The glory of the Lord staves him off. Sometimes, when "the cloud covered the tent of meeting, and the glory of the LORD filled the tabernacle" (40:34), Moses couldn't enter. God's glory is so substantial, even in the form of a cloud, that there's simply no room for anyone or anything else.

But still the cloud doesn't leave. God remains faithful and present, even if obscure and unapproachable. "Throughout all their journeys, whenever the cloud was taken up from over the tabernacle, the people of Israel would set out. But if the cloud was not taken up, then they did not set out till the day that it was taken up. For the cloud of the LORD was on the tabernacle by day, and fire was in it by night, in the sight of all the house of Israel throughout all their journeys" (40:36–38).

The Book of Exodus ends under that cloud.

The memory of the cloud was precious to Israel. It is recalled and remembered again and again, from Exodus's near-neighbor of Numbers, to much-further-off Nehemiah, to assorted Psalms.

The descent of the infilling cloud is the confirmation that Solomon's temple has pleased the Lord. "When the priests came out of the Holy Place, a cloud filled the house of the LORD, so that the priests could not stand to minister because of the cloud, for the glory of the LORD filled the house of the LORD" (I Kings 8:10–11, cf. II Chronicles 5:13–14). Cloud and glory and local-personal Presence all coincide again in the temple.

Yet there is, at the same time, a competing narrative of God-in-the-cloud. It points up the ambivalence of the cloud imagery, already on view in Genesis 9, where a rainbow in the clouds reminds God of his covenant with Noah never again to destroy the earth. The cloud may shed life-giving rain, but it may also shed a death-dealing flood.

The competing cloud narrative also serves an apologetic purpose, not to say a polemical one, putting the LORD God of Israel in direct competition with that pretender to the throne, the rain god Baal who rides the clouds—or so he claims, or so his false prophets claim.

Thus Elijah confronts the blasphemous claims of Baal and his myrmidons by withholding rain and bestowing fire instead. It's only after the fiery consumption of Baal's altar that the true Lord of rain allows it to fall once more.

But in general, it's hard to argue with a storm. It's better to seize the power of the storm and reassign it to the one who actually deserves the credit.

These two aspects of the cloud are merged as early as Deuteronomy 5:22, when Moses says, "These words the LORD spoke to all your assembly at the mountain out of the midst of the fire, the cloud, and the thick darkness, with a loud voice." "Clouds and thick darkness" in time becomes a commonplace of prophetic literature, popping up in Ezekiel 34:12, Joel 2:2, and Zephaniah 1:15, and in Psalm 97:2 as well.

David in a song of deliverance testifies that the Lord "made darkness around him his canopy, thick clouds, a gathering of water. Out of the brightness before him coals of fire flamed forth. The LORD thundered from heaven, and the Most High uttered his voice. And he sent out arrows and scattered them; lightning, and routed them" (II Samuel 22:12–15, cf. Psalm 18:11–14).[24]

In Isaiah the two associations with the cloud, as protective covering and as wrathful storm, coexist in tension. In the first case, "Then the LORD will create over the whole site of Mount Zion and over her assemblies a cloud by day, and smoke and the shining of a flaming fire by night; for over all the glory there will be a canopy. There will be a booth [*sukkah!*] for shade by day from the heat, and for a refuge and a shelter from the storm and rain" (4:5–6), and "I have blotted out your transgressions like a cloud and your sins like mist; return to me, for I have redeemed you" (44:22).

In the second case, "Behold, the LORD is riding on a swift cloud" (19:1), and "The LORD will cause his majestic voice to be heard and the descending blow of his arm to be seen, in furious anger and a flame of devouring fire, with a cloudburst and storm and hailstones" (30:30).

Storm god imagery hails down also in Nahum. "The LORD is a jealous and avenging God; the LORD is avenging and wrathful; the LORD takes vengeance on his adversaries and keeps wrath for his enemies. The LORD is slow to anger and great in power, and the LORD will by no means clear the guilty. His way is in whirlwind and storm, and the clouds are the dust of his feet. He rebukes the sea and makes it dry; he dries up all the rivers; Bashan and Carmel wither; the bloom of Lebanon withers. The mountains quake before him; the hills melt; the earth heaves before him, the world and all who dwell in it" (1:2–5).

All this is a further clue to the summoning of James and John, sons of Zebedee, to the mountain of Transfiguration. For they incline toward calling down fire, hoping to see the Lord in action as a storm god.

On the mountaintop, the Sons of Thunder finally get their chance to walk right into the heart of the cloud. They find there, however, neither whirlwind nor hailstones—but a voice.

In Mark, the action comes fast and thick. First they hike up the mountain. Then Jesus is transfigured. Then Elijah and Moses appear. Then those two engage Jesus in conversation. Then Peter, terrified, interrupts with his foolish chatter. And then a cloud comes to be overshadowing (*episkiázousa*) them.

It's a rare word, "overshadowing," though fitting for the subject. Everyone's had the experience of walking along on a sunny day and suddenly registering gloom and darkness. You look up to see that a cloud has passed in front of the sun, casting an uncanny shadow.

But of course, the word is not only precise to the meteorological event. It's also scripturally evocative. In the Septuagint translation of the last chapter of Exodus, and in nearly the last verse, we are told, "And the cloud hid the tabernacle [*skēnē̂*] of witness, and the tabernacle was filled by the glory of the LORD; and Moses could not enter into the tabernacle of witness, because the cloud overshadowed [*epeskíazen*] it and the tabernacle was filled by the glory of the LORD" (40:34–35).[25]

Matthew seems to blend the pillar of fire with the pillar of cloud to achieve a *phōteinḕ*, "bright," cloud (17:5). The adjective derives from the noun for light, *phōs*. *Phōs* is the root of "photo" but makes its most suggestive appearance in English as the element phosphorus, from Greek for "light-bearer," so named because white phosphorus glows when exposed to oxygen. The *phōteinḕ* cloud gestures to the transfigured Jesus, whose clothes became "white like light [*phōs*]." The light of Jesus and the light of God in the cloud are one and the same light.

At this point you might well rush to Peter's defense. Cloud overshadowing, glory of the Lord, light eternal? See, it *is* time for tabernacles!

True, but which kind of tabernacle? Peter jumped the gun, offering to build booths *before* the cloud overshadowed in evocation of the Exodus tabernacle. And *that* tabernacle is not for Sukkot, but for the Lord's dwelling near to, if not quite in the midst of, his people. The correct association of images and actions aligns Jesus himself with the tabernacle of witness upon which the Presence of the Lord settles—a point that John develops in his own Gospel.

Luke took a different sort of inspiration from Mark's account of the Transfiguration. In *his* Gospel, the word "overshadow" makes exactly one other appearance: when the angel Gabriel informs the maiden Mary just how these things might be since she has never known a man. "The Holy Spirit will come upon you, and the power of the Most High will overshadow [*episkiásei*] you; therefore the child to be born will be called holy—the Son of God" (1:35).[26]

Note the connections: the Holy Spirit *and* the Most High, distinguished in person yet united in action, the latter in particular overshadowing Mary like the cloud overshadowed the tabernacle, will bring about the holy child. The Virgin and the mountain of Transfiguration alike are chosen as unique sites of the Lord's overshadowing. The result in both cases is a holy and beloved son, son of Mary, Son of God.

Here at last we bump up against one of the central mysteries of the Transfiguration.

Jesus' appearance is altered; he goes from the ordinary form of humanity to an extraordinary figure of glory, gleaming and dazzling white like lightning.

But he is *silent.*

The Presence that has accompanied Israel for so long appears in one of its most familiar forms, the overshadowing cloud. There is nothing particularly unusual about its appearance.

But the Presence *speaks.*

Up till now Jesus has spoken, and abundantly. His ministry is characterized by preaching and teaching. He proclaims repentance for the forgiveness of sins and the kingdom of God. He announces and enacts, by his words, that forgiveness and that kingdom. The crowds are every bit as astonished by his speaking as they are by his casting out of demons and healing of the sick, for he speaks as one with authority and not like one of their scribes.

Silence has not characterized Jesus' ministry up to this point in time, except on one other occasion.

Meanwhile, the ubiquitous hiddenness, the aloof nearness, has stayed in the background. It has not spoken publicly since Mount

Sinai. Ever since retreating to the tabernacle of witness, that Presence has spoken only and always through mediators, first Moses, then the prophets, "lest I consume you."

Speech has not characterized the Presence up to this point in Jesus' ministry, except on one other occasion.

In the Gospels of Mark and John, baptism is the very first thing to talk about regarding Jesus' ministry. In Matthew and Luke, a backstory sets the stage for baptism. Yet all four Evangelists agree that Jesus' ministry of speaking, teaching, and preaching is not inaugurated apart from and until John's ministry of baptizing.

"In those days," Mark explains, "Jesus came from Nazareth of Galilee and was baptized by John in the Jordan. And when he came up out of the water, immediately he saw the heavens being torn open and the Spirit descending on him like a dove. And a voice came from heaven, 'You are my beloved Son; with you I am well pleased'" (1:9–11).

Other than the introductory gloss, this is the first naming of Jesus, nine verses in. The Lord God has been named in the quotation from the prophets (1:3). The Holy Spirit has been named in John's announcement of one who will baptize with more-than-water (1:8).

But in Mark's telling, Jesus neither appears nor says nor does anything until his Baptism. More than that, Jesus neither says nor does anything *during* his Baptism. The one who will go on to effect astounding miracles is entirely passive here, entirely the recipient, the object and not the subject. It is by being the object of the action that he can be become the subject of the action, after the voice from heaven tells him who he is: *You are my beloved Son.*

This is remarkable enough where Jesus is concerned, this Jesus who has done nothing to earn or prove his new moniker. But what can slip by unnoticed is how even *more* remarkable it is where the voice from heaven is concerned.

Definitionally, there cannot be a son without there also being a parent. If Jesus is named as Son, then the voice from heaven is equally confessing something about itself. God is no longer simply "God." It is inadequate and insufficiently specific as a term anymore. If the voice from heaven names Jesus as Son, beloved Son, Son of—we cannot avoid it—*God*, then "God" as a term must be amplified in recognition of Jesus' Sonship.

This is such a startling development in the Israelite doctrine of God that Jesus holds back from inflicting its full implications on his hearers until they have been inducted into the equally startling development in the Israelite doctrine of the Messiah. It's only after Jesus teaches for the first time that the Son *of Man* must suffer and be put to death (Mark 8:31) that he draws out the full consequences of his Sonship. "For whoever is ashamed of me and of my words in this adulterous and sinful generation, of him will the Son of Man also be ashamed when he comes in the glory of his *Father* with the holy angels" (8:38).

Here for the first time in Mark's Gospel, God is named and specified as *Father*.

The very next thing that happens is the Transfiguration.

Matthew preserves Mark's account of Jesus' Baptism almost unaltered, except for adding a quarrel between the two men about whether John should baptize Jesus instead of the other way around. Luke wants to dissociate Christian baptism from John's baptism so radically that he interrupts Mark's account of the scene at the Jordan to lock John up in prison. Luke then resumes the narrative, getting Jesus baptized without identifying a baptizer.

All four Gospels report that the Spirit of God descends on Jesus "like a dove," though the Synoptics specify the moment as when Jesus rises up out of the water, while John is hazy about the exact timing or whether, in fact, Jesus ever gets baptized at all. The most notable predecessor to the baptismal dove is the dove after the flood. This dove links the dark side of the storm god with the bright side of the rainbow through the medium of the cloud.

But at the Baptism of Jesus there is no cloud, only "heaven" and the voice that speaks from it. At this point it is hardly necessary to get more specific than heaven: we know perfectly well who's doing the talking here. We also see firsthand the distinguished-not-divided, unique-yet-united Persons of God-the-Father-in-heaven who speaks and acts first and sends the other two, the Son who is begotten and born and receives in order to respond and act, and the Holy Spirit who both passively is sent and actively descends. It is no casual or forced reading that brought the church from its earliest days to see in this Baptism nothing less than the holy Trinity, one God.

Mark, and Luke following him, depict this tableau as an internal conversation. We are privileged to eavesdrop, but it is more for Jesus' benefit than for ours. The voice from heaven announces in the second person, "*You are* my beloved Son." Then, in the first person, still in direct address to Jesus: "With you I am well pleased."

Matthew shifts to observer status, with the voice announcing to anyone *other* than Jesus, "*This is* my beloved Son, with *whom* I am well pleased." Still, Matthew preserves Mark's positioning of Jesus as the primary observer, with both Evangelists reporting how *Jesus* saw the Spirit of God descending upon him like a dove. John's Gospel pulls farthest back, with the Baptizer reporting after the fact how *he* saw the Spirit like a dove descending on a Jesus whom he did not yet recognize.

As is the cloud to Exodus, so is the voice of the Lord to Deuteronomy. Its first appearance does not bode well.

Moses is recalling the events at Horeb/Sinai to the people. The Lord gathered them so that they might hear his words and teach them to their children. "And you came near and stood at the foot of the mountain, while the mountain burned with fire to the heart of heaven, wrapped in darkness, cloud, and gloom. Then the LORD spoke to you out of the midst of the fire. You heard the sound of words, but saw no form; there was only a voice" (4:11–12). The voice now takes precedence over the cloud as it pronounces the Ten Commandments.

In the next chapter, Moses undertakes to repeat those Ten Commandments, concluding, "These words the LORD spoke to all your assembly at the mountain out of the midst of the fire, the cloud, and the thick darkness, with a loud voice" (5:22). He reminds the Israelites of how they were politely appreciative of the manifestation of the Lord's glory and greatness, but ultimately judged the voice of the Lord more threat than comfort. "If we hear the voice of the LORD our God any more, we shall die! For who is there of all flesh, that has heard the voice of the living God speaking out of the midst of fire as we have, and has still lived?" (5:25–26, cf. 18:16). So they begged Moses to stand in as their mediator. God didn't disagree.

From this point onward, the context of the "voice of the LORD" is the command to obey it. Obey the voice of the Lord, and you will prosper. Disobey or shut your ears to the voice of the Lord, and so much the worse for you. It is Deuteronomy's constant refrain: obey the voice, the voice of the Lord.

By the time we get to Israel's first king, the covenant has already fallen apart. First Samuel is a contest of obedience to competing voices. Eli's sons will not obey his voice. The Lord urges Samuel to obey the voice of the people despite their preferring a human king over a divine king. The people in turn refuse to obey Samuel's voice urging them to reconsider. Samuel tries one more time to warn them, deuteronomistically, "If you will fear the LORD and serve him and obey his voice and not rebel against the commandment of the LORD, and if both you and the king who reigns over you will follow the LORD your God, it will be well. But if you will not obey the voice of the LORD, but rebel against the commandment of the LORD, then the hand of the LORD will be against you and your king" (12:14–15). Of course, they disobey. Meanwhile Saul falsely brags to have obeyed the voice of the Lord, but his actual disobedience costs him the kingship.

At the far end of the kingdom, Jeremiah unfolds at length the devastating consequences of long-term disobedience to the voice of the Lord. He recalls again and again the covenant: *if only* you had obeyed the voice of the Lord! He recalls again and again the history: how they *never* obeyed the voice of the Lord! Since they would not have the Lord's voice, other voices shall be silenced as well. "I will banish from them the voice of mirth and the voice of gladness, the voice of the bridegroom and the voice of the bride, the grinding of the millstones and the light of the lamp" (25:10). The Lord will cease to woo with them his voice, uttering henceforth only destruction: "The LORD will roar from on high, and from his holy habitation utter his voice; he will roar mightily against his fold, and shout, like those who tread grapes, against all the inhabitants of the earth" (25:30).

And yet, Israel can expect reprieve in the end. Whereas toward Babylon, which destroyed at God's command and yet will be destroyed for its destructiveness, the Lord will fully inhabit the mask of the storm god. Within an oracle of Babylon's downfall, Jeremiah testifies, "When he utters his voice there is a tumult of waters in the heavens, and he makes the mist rise from the ends of the earth. He makes lightning for the rain, and he brings forth the wind from his storehouses" (50:16).

Above all, it is Psalm 29 that unites the Lord's two ways of being cloaked in the clouds with his voice. Inviting the heavenly beings to ascribe, the Lord's glory, strength, splendor, and holiness are singled out. Then comes a sequence of testimonies regarding the Lord's voice: "The voice of the LORD is over the waters; the God of glory thunders, the LORD, over many waters. The voice of the LORD is powerful; the voice of the LORD is full of majesty. The voice of the LORD breaks the cedars... The voice of the LORD flashes forth flames of fire. The voice of the LORD shakes the wilderness... The voice of the LORD makes the deer give birth and strips the forests bare, and in his temple all cry, 'Glory!' The LORD sits enthroned over the flood; the LORD sits enthroned as king forever. May the LORD give strength to his people! May the LORD bless his people with peace!"

Lord of the storm, Lord of blessing: one Lord, one glory, one voice. It is almost as though this Psalm is preparing us for the Transfiguration.

The author of Second Peter might well have thought so. For while he speaks of the holy mountain, he says nothing of the cloud. And while he claims his status as eyewitness, he says nothing of what his eye might have seen. Nothing about clothing, face, or appearance. Nothing that is white as light or dazzling as lightning.

In Second Peter, the voice takes precedence over all else. The invisible voice, twice mentioned (1:17, 18), is nevertheless a thing of "splendor" (1:16). It conveys "honor and glory" to the Son from the "majestic glory" (1:17). It is a direct address of "heaven" (1:18) to earth, and of the Father to the Son. For in this Epistle, beyond the habitual reserve of Mark and even the expansive interpretations of

Matthew and Luke, the author explicitly draws out the inference of the startling development in the Israelite doctrine of God. It is no longer adequate or accurate to say that God, simple and unqualified "God," spoke from heaven to Jesus on the holy mountain. To identify God correctly, the God of the Gospel, we must now say that "God Father" spoke to "my Son, my beloved."

This development in the Israelite doctrine of God had already become standard in the Christian doctrine of God. The very first (still extant) work of Christian literature, so far as we know, is Paul's First Epistle to the Thessalonians. As he writes in his opening address, "We give thanks to God always for all of you, constantly mentioning you in our prayers, remembering before our God and Father your work of faith and labor of love and steadfastness of hope in our Lord Jesus Christ" (1:2–3). The first mention of "God" is promptly glossed by the second, "God and Father," who is so with respect to the one mentioned at the end of the sentence, "our Lord Jesus Christ."

And just in case, say, some future church council will get as far as the divinity of the Son but still needs to wrestle with the divinity of the Spirit, Paul in considerate anticipation continues, "For we know, brothers loved by God, that he has chosen you, because our gospel came to you not only in word, but also in power and in the Holy Spirit and with full conviction" (1:4–5).

But that is a modification of the doctrine of God for another time.

In the Baptism of Jesus, Father speaks to Son while others overhear or watch from the sidelines.

At the Transfiguration, the Father speaks to everyone *except* Jesus.

Here all the Evangelists and eyewitnesses accord in their reporting. God the Father speaks and says, "*This is* my Son." Jesus knows who he is. The problem is whether anyone else does, especially since he's started talking about the cross. A baptized, well-pleasing Son of God was reasonably easy to believe in. A soon-to-be-suffering, certainly-to-be-crucified Son of God is considerably harder to believe in. The timing of the Transfiguration speaks not so much to a development in Jesus' self-understanding, but to the crisis in the disciples' Christ-understanding.

Which brings us back again, sideways and indirectly, to the Transfiguration that does not take place in the Gospel of John. "He who sent me" (1:33) tells John the Baptizer privately about the identity of Jesus who will baptize with the Holy Spirit, but this is not a public sermon. Onlookers have only the Baptizer's word to go by.

Over the next eleven chapters, Jesus speaks often and at length about who he is—*I AM*, he says, the bread of life, the light of the world, the good shepherd, the resurrection and the life—and about who God is: chiefly, his Father. But this Father does not confirm the Son's claim on him. Jesus paradoxically admits as much. "The Father who sent me has himself borne witness about me. His voice you have never heard, his form you have never seen" (5:37).

Jesus' interlocutors are understandably skeptical. "You are bearing witness about yourself; your testimony is not true... Where is your Father?" (8:13, 19). Jesus counters that if they truly knew his Father, they'd know him, and vice versa. But anyone could say that. How is Jesus not just another pretender to the divine throne?

Only after every pilgrimage festival has been celebrated and Hanukkah besides, only after Jesus demonstrates his power over death with the raising of Lazarus, and only after some Gentiles catch wind of Jesus' ministry and come curiously inquiring after him—only then does the divine Father disclose himself.

It happens like this. A large crowd greets Jesus as he enters Jerusalem, waving branches of palm trees and crying "Hosanna!" (12:13). It's Sukkot behavior, even though they all know perfectly well that they've come to the city for Passover. Peter wasn't the only one to get befuddled on the festival timeline. John notes that even the disciples didn't understand until after Jesus had been "glorified" (12:16). Of course not: Sukkot imagery makes sense in the light of glory, but not in the light of suffering.

Then, "some Greeks" (12:20) show up in Jerusalem for the Passover festival. You may recall the earlier confusion at the Feast of Tabernacles: "Does he intend to go to the Dispersion among the Greeks and teach the Greeks?" (7:35). Well, it turns out the Greeks came to him instead. They inform Philip that they "wish to see Jesus" (12:21). Philip and Andrew convey the message to the master.

Jesus promptly replies, "The hour has come for the Son of Man to be glorified" (12:23)—the exact opposite of his response to his mother's request to do something about the wine running out back in Cana. In a Gospel utterly unperturbed by Gentile faith in the Messiah, it's notable that foreigners' interest in Jesus proves to be the trigger for the final act. The time has come, and is now, for Jesus to face his cross.

At this precise moment, John gives us the Garden of Gethsemane and the Transfiguration packaged into a single exchange, which is, moreover, the one and only time in this Gospel that the Father speaks directly, from heaven, and in public.

Jesus says, "Now is my soul troubled. And what shall I say? 'Father, save me from this hour'? But for this purpose I have come to this hour. Father, glorify your name."

This time, the Father responds. "Then a voice came from heaven: 'I have glorified it, and I will glorify it again'" (12:28). Voice, heaven, glory. And eyewitnesses, or more precisely *ear*witnesses, though even less reliable than Peter, James, and John. "The crowd that stood there and heard it said that it had thundered." Thunder! "Others said, 'An angel has spoken to him.'"

Jesus corrects them and explains why, at last, his Father has spoken up. "This voice has come for your sake, not mine. Now is the judgment of this world; now will the ruler of this world be cast out. And I, when I am lifted up from the earth, will draw all people to myself" (12:32).

But again there cannot, must not, will not ever be talk of his glory and exaltation apart from his cross. "He said this to show by what kind of death he was going to die" (12:33).

Which points us to the other notable appearance of the cloud in the New Testament.

We are on the other side of the cross. We are even on the other side of the Resurrection. We are gazing upon the face of Jesus for the very last time.

"As they were looking on, he was lifted up, and a cloud took him out of their sight. And while they were gazing into heaven as he went, behold, two men stood by them in white robes, and said, 'Men of Galilee, why do you stand looking into heaven? This Jesus, who was taken up from you into heaven, will come in the same way as you saw him go into heaven'" (Acts 1:9–11).

As the cloud marked the Presence that named Jesus as beloved Son, so the cloud marks the Presence that receives the ascending Jesus back into heaven. But not forever. He will come again in the same way as they saw him go.

All Israelite ears well-versed in the Scriptures would have pricked up at this; they'd catch the allusion to Daniel at once. "I saw in the night visions, and behold, with the clouds of heaven there came one like a son of man, and he came to the Ancient of Days and was presented before him" (7:13). Apart from Exodus, this is by far the most influential cloud image to shape the New Testament imagination (cf. Matthew 24:30, 26:64; Mark 13:26, 14:62; Luke 21:27; Revelation 1:7, 14:14–16).

What with the cloud and the voice from heaven, the mutual identification of Father and Son, and the rule of three setting up expectations of what should follow Jesus' Baptism and Transfiguration, we naturally look for a confirmatory repetition of the pattern at the Resurrection.

But when Jesus is raised from the dead, there is no light, no glory, no cloud, no voice, no naming.

Why not?

II Peter 1:16-18

16 For not having imitated
sophisticated myths,

we made known to you all
the power and parousia
of our Lord Jesus Christ,

rather having come to be
eyewitnesses
of that splendor.

17 For accepting
from God Father
honor and glory
from such a voice
having been borne to him
by the majestic glory:

This is
my Son,
my beloved,
in whom
I
take pleasure—

18 And we
heard this voice
having been borne from heaven,
being with him
in the holy mountain.

Parousia : My Son, My Beloved

In Jesus' Baptism and Transfiguration there is a common pattern: the miraculous action is performed upon him rather than by him. He is object, not subject. He is the only-begotten Son who receives from his almighty Father. He is passive in order to be active, spoken-over in order to speak, and the order of the in-order-to makes all the difference.

But in Jesus' Resurrection, there is a change in the pattern. One might even say, a metamorphosis.

The culmination of the story in both the Baptism and the Transfiguration is the speech from heaven or the cloud. Either way, from the Lord God who qualifies himself as Father.

Mark reports the speech from the cloud on the mountain as, "This is my Son, the beloved [*agapētós*]; listen to him" (9:7). Matthew expands slightly with a phrase that all three Evangelists report at the Baptism, "This is my Son, the beloved, in whom I take pleasure; listen to him" (17:5). Luke moves farthest from the language of the Baptism, changing the modifier of Son: "This is my Son, the one who has been chosen; listen to him" (9:35).

The middle phrase differs, but the three Synoptics are in total agreement as to the opening and closing of the voice's speech about Jesus at the Transfiguration.

"This is my Son." There is such a wealth of son-imagery across the Old Testament that the word doesn't and can't prove much in isolation. It was natural enough to designate a merely human king as God's son: "The LORD said to me, 'You are my Son; today I have begotten you'" (Psalm 2:7). It is only in the light of many other facts about Jesus that this royal Psalm for a Davidic king takes on messianic and ultimately trinitarian significance. Yet it matters, and has always mattered, that the anointed one, the Christ, was a royal figure—

however you choose to upset conventional notions of kingly rule, such as by placing a crown of thorns upon the king's head.

Adding the detail that this Son of God is "beloved" already starts that process. Attentive ears would have recognized the words of the angel to Abraham: "Take your son, your only son Isaac, whom you love, and go to the land of Moriah, and offer him there as a burnt offering on one of the mountains of which I shall tell you" (Genesis 22:2). Son, only son, well-loved son, son offered as sacrifice. Once again the Septuagint makes a level path for the Evangelists by replacing "only" with "beloved," so that the angel commands Abraham, "Take your son, the beloved [agapētón]."[27] The same set of associations packs the punch in the parable of the tenants who murder the vineyard-owner's "beloved son" in Mark 12:6.

Since it has already been established at the Baptism that Jesus is beloved, Luke takes a different tack for clarifying the nature of the royal Son's kingship. He thinks not of Isaac in Genesis but of the Lord's servant in Isaiah, who is repeatedly called "chosen." "Behold my servant, whom I uphold, my chosen, in whom my soul delights; I have put my Spirit upon him; he will bring forth justice to the nations" (42:1; cf. 41:8–9, 43:10, 44:1). Matthew agrees with both the allusion and the choosing, but reserves it for another occasion (12:15–21). Needless to say, you don't have to travel much further into Isaiah for that servant to start suffering.

Beloved, pleasing, and chosen, but above all, *Son*, "my Son," God's Son. Jesus regularly speaks of himself as "the Son of Man," a phrase that can be anthropologically generic (as in the Psalms and Ezekiel) or apocalyptically fraught (as in Daniel). Other people regularly speak of Jesus as "the son of David," another case of not really knowing what they're saying—too little and too much at the same time.

But when Mark, in particular, allows the utterance "Son of God," we ought to snap to attention. If we bracket out the phrase in 1:1 (and its uncertain textual history), the first acknowledgement of Jesus as *God's* Son takes place at the Baptism. Evidently the human auditors can make no sense of this claim, because never once do they repeat it. Indeed, for the rest of Jesus' earthly life, only the demons recognize him for who he is. "And whenever the unclean spirits saw him, they fell down before him and cried out, 'You are the Son of God'" (3:11). "And crying out with a loud voice, he said, 'What have you to do with me, Jesus, Son of the Most High God? I adjure you by God, do not torment me'" (5:7).

Two demonic attestations set against one divine attestation is a bad ratio. The Transfiguration makes it a tie, two and two. The final irony of Mark's Gospel is that the tiebreaking vote goes to the Roman centurion who oversaw the Crucifixion: "Truly this man was the Son of God!" (15:39).

Though what good did it do Jesus, in the end, to be the Son of God?

On the other side of the declaration that Jesus is the Son of God is the command, "Listen to him." On the immediate and obvious level, it is a reminder of the promise made to Moses in Deuteronomy 18:15, "The LORD your God will raise up for you a prophet like me from among you, from your brothers—it is to him you shall listen" (cf. Acts 3:22). Moses's amiable attendance at Jesus' party shores up the association.

Yet press a little further beyond the obvious, and two surprising realizations swiftly follow.

First, it is extraordinarily unusual for the Presence to speak. Human ears would naturally tune in to the voice from the cloud, astounded that it is speaking and they are hearing. In equal measure, it is not a little astounding that the vocable, authoritative Jesus is silent here, not saying anything at all. So how *could* one listen to him?

Clearly the moment refers beyond itself. God-the-Father-in-heaven underscores his beloved Son's rightness in speaking of the cross and suffering, and commands the disciples to keep on listening as the Son keeps on speaking of these things.

Yet the irony remains: listen to the one who is not speaking, on the spoken authority of the one who almost never speaks. It is not intended as a contradiction, but as a transfer of identity based on divine love ("the beloved") and divine choice ("the one who has been chosen").

Second, out of all the extraordinary events that the disciples are commanded to retain from this experience, it is *not* what they have *seen.* Even Second Peter grasps the oddity of this truth. While defending the disciples' status as "eyewitnesses," the author describes nothing of what Peter and the other two beheld. No luminous face, no dazzling garments, not even a bright cloud!

What the eyewitnesses later report, in fact, is only what they have *heard.* In truth, they are *earwitnesses.* And *they* are earwitnesses only because *Jesus* is the first and foremost earwitness: "For accepting from God Father honor and glory from such a voice having been borne to him by the majestic glory: This is my Son, my beloved, in whom I take pleasure" (1:17).

In Second Peter's telling of the Transfiguration, there are two subtle intensifications of the intimacy between the Father and the Son. For one, the voice from heaven declares this to be "my Son, *my* beloved," not just "*the* beloved." It isn't grammatically necessary to say "my" twice; once would have done the trick. But this Father insists on the figure in question being both "*my* Son" and "*my* beloved," doubly claimed.

Then, after the Father declares pleasure in his Son, another grammatically unnecessary personal pronoun sounds forth: "in whom *I* take pleasure." This is the Greek *ego,* same word as the Freudian "ego," the first-person singular pronoun "I," already implied by the verb form and therefore usually left out. It's left out in the Synoptics. It's included here to stress the point, as in Jesus' *I AM* sayings.

Thus speaks the Father, knowing that the Son is overhearing an address ostensibly meant for others. Only afterwards does Second Peter turn to the disciples' experience of this speech: "And we heard this voice having been borne from heaven, being with him in the holy mountain" (1:18). It is as if, knowing the problems of describing glory, Second Peter has abandoned the effort—but the difficulty serves his larger purpose well.

Peter may have been an eyewitness, but you, reader, are not. In all likelihood Second Peter's actual author was not, either. And after all, only three of the twelve disciples were eyewitnesses. *Seeing* the transfigured Jesus was never central to the unfolding plan of God's mighty act of salvation.

What matters is to listen—and by the time of the writing of Second

Peter, that was so obviously true he didn't even have to repeat the command. If it is no longer possible to see the face of Jesus, transfigured or otherwise, what else *can* you do but listen to his word?

Yet even this isn't the whole story. The voice from heaven commands the disciples to *listen*. But the no-longer-transfigured Jesus shifts attention back to what they have *seen*. In Mark, "he charged them that they describe what they *saw* to not one single person, until when the Son of Man should rise from the dead" (9:9). It is the familiar messianic secret, but this time with an expiration date.

Matthew emphasizes even more than Mark the visual character of the whole experience. "Jesus commanded them, saying: Tell the *vision* to not one single person until when the Son of Man should be raised from the dead" (17:9). In Luke, the disciples voluntarily hold their tongues, but again with specific reference to what they saw. "And they kept silent and announced to nobody in those days anything that they had *seen*" (9:36).

Whether Jesus had to say so or not, all three Evangelists agree that the Transfiguration cannot be understood rightly before and until the Resurrection. And yet, as noted earlier, there is a stunning lack of correspondence between the transfigured Jesus and the risen Jesus. The latter's face is not immediately recognized; other people are the ones to wear the bright white clothes; there is no light or glory; and there is decidedly no voice from heaven. In fact, in Mark, there isn't only no voice from heaven; there's no Jesus! "He has been raised; he is not here," says the young man in a white robe to the frightened women (16:6).[28]

We are driven to conclude that, while the Transfiguration cannot be understood rightly apart from the Resurrection, it is nevertheless not the same kind of thing as the Resurrection. Seeing the transfigured Jesus did *not* illuminate the disciples as to "what it is, to rise from the dead" (9:10). The distinction between the two is important, even essential, to understanding either. Our final task is to sort out what, precisely, that difference is.

The first clue comes from the verb that *doesn't* get used.

Metamorphóō, to change or transform or transfigure or metamorphose, is the verb of choice for Jesus' mountaintop alteration. But it is *never* applied to the risen Jesus. For all the difficulty in recognizing the risen Jesus—which, we are given to believe, has more to do with spiritual blockage than a confusing countenance—the emphasis is laid on the continuity of identity between the one who was crucified and the one who has risen. Strange as it sounds, Jesus was not *changed* by his death. He is one and the same Jesus before and after his death and Resurrection.

And so, by extension, the *metamorphóō* verb is never applied to the dead who are raised in Christ, either. As we've seen, Paul knows the verb and uses it where spiritual transformation is concerned. But he doesn't deploy it in his extended meditation on the bodily resurrection. "We shall be changed" (*allagēsómetha*)—but not transfigured (I Corinthians 15:51, 52).

Thus the first major distinction: a transfigured body does not have to die first. A risen body does. There is no resurrection apart from death.

That tells us what made witnessing the Transfiguration more a danger for the disciples than a privilege. Peter saw in it what anyone would have seen: a glorification apart from suffering, cross, and death; a skipping over painful Passover to land in the neverending celebration of Sukkot. That is why the Transfiguration had to be framed so tightly by Passion predictions, and why the three eyewitnesses had to be warned so sternly not to talk about what they'd seen until *after* Jesus' Resurrection, and thus of course not until *after* Jesus' death.

Matthew uniquely signals this connection. When the voice from heaven speaks, the disciples fall on their faces in terror. Jesus, back to normal, approaches and "fastens on" to them—a stronger verb than a simple touch. As he fastens on to them, he speaks two commands of his own: "Be raised and fear not" (9:7). The latter makes good sense; we've been told how frightened the disciples were. And the former makes sense for people laid out flat by terror.

But something more hides behind this command. What Jesus says is *egérthēte*, a passive imperative derived from *egeírō*, one of the two verbs used with respect to resurrection. It needn't carry any extra meaning; it can just mean "to raise" or "to lift," as you'd do with a book lying on a table. That usage appears in the New Testament with no double entendre intended.

Yet two verses later, in the conclusion to Matthew's Transfiguration story, this verb appears again in all its resounding significance. "Tell the vision to not one single person until when the Son of Man is raised [*egerthê*] from the dead" (17:9). Neither Mark nor Luke felt the need to mention how Jesus raised the disciples, much less by means of a resurrection verb. It's hard to take the double appearance of this verb as sheer coincidence.

Matthew makes it clear: understanding cannot come to the disciples until Jesus has been raised—but also, not until they have been raised by Jesus.

Mark closes out the Transfiguration scene with puzzlement—not the first time he's made that move, nor will it be the last. In response to Jesus' charge to keep silent until afterwards, the three disciples "held back the word to themselves, disputing what it is, to rise from the dead" (9:10).

They are right to be puzzled. Hope for resurrection was certainly in the air at their time and place. But it was taken for granted that, if and when resurrection happened, it would be general and collective. Or, even if only of a select group such as the righteous, then all of them at once. And when it happened, it would mark the end. Resurrection would mean that history had wound down and drawn to a close. What nobody was expecting at all was, first, the resurrection of one single person all by himself, and, second, that history would keep trucking along afterwards.

Paul had to deal with ongoing confusion over Jesus' Resurrection in his Corinthian congregation. He keeps explaining to them that the risen Jesus is the beginning of something, not the end. "Christ has been raised from the dead, the firstfruits [*aparchê*] of those who have fallen asleep" (I Corinthians 15:20). His choice of word is weighty: a sign that Passover has ended and it's time for the next festival.

It is time, in fact, for Pentecost.

While Christians tend to forget Sukkot altogether, we do remember Pentecost. What we forget about Pentecost, though, is that it was a Jewish festival long before it became a Christian one. We read the opening line of Acts 2 as if it were a redundant statement of fact, a festival tautology. "When the day of Pentecost arrived," so did the Holy Spirit, because the Holy Spirit arrives on Pentecost, because Pentecost is the festival of the Holy Spirit!

Further, by not remembering Pentecost as a Jewish festival first, we misinterpret the roll call of nations—"Parthians and Medes and Elamites and residents of Mesopotamia" and so forth—as a reference to Gentiles, at long last included in the supposedly exclusivistic people of God. But this utterly misreads both Acts 2 and the history of Pentecost up to this point, not to mention the Lord God's longstanding concern for peoples outside the covenant.

It is still Jews and only Jews in Acts 2. At the furthest stretch, there are some "proselytes"—but that means fully observant converts. The vast majority of those present are diaspora Jews who have traveled to Jerusalem precisely because Pentecost is the second of the mandated pilgrimage festivals. The miracle of tongues is not that the Jewish apostles became intelligible to foreigners, but that the Jewish apostles communicated with fellow Jews who have lived so far away, for so long, that Jerusalem's local language of Aramaic and religious language of Hebrew are nothing but babble to them.

The nations will, of course, get grafted in. But not yet. Not on Pentecost. The ingrafting begins in Acts 8 with the Samaritans, those northern Israelites who, through much compromise and intermingling, lived on after the Assyrian conquest and came to prefer their local Mount Gerizim to the Judeans' Mount Zion. After them we'll have an Ethiopian proselyte. The breakthrough to the Gentiles will occur only in Acts 10, when Peter (against his better judgment) is sent by God to a Roman centurion, whose household receives the Holy Spirit and bursts into tongues of praise before Peter can even finish his sermon.

So what happens on the day of Pentecost is by no means the completed church of all the nations, much less the eschatological harvest. On Pentecost the Spirit gathers up the firstfruits: the first ones to believe in Jesus after his Resurrection from among his own people. The Jews who believed in him beforehand—the disciples and Mary and his brothers and a few others besides—are the ones who undertake this first harvest, by the power of the Holy Spirit poured out upon them.

Of course this happens on Pentecost. Pentecost *is* the festival of firstfruits!

Pentecost is first mentioned in Exodus 23, right in between the first mentions of Passover and Sukkot, though it's not immediately obvious to a reader in English. "You shall keep the Feast of Harvest, of the firstfruits of your labor, of what you sow in the field" (v. 16). It appears a second time with the second announcement of the three festivals, now clearly designated as pilgrimage festivals, in Exodus 34: "You shall observe the Feast of Weeks, the firstfruits of wheat harvest" (v. 22; cf. Deuteronomy 16:16, II Chronicles 8:12).

Already you can see the variation in terminology: the Feast of Harvest and Feast of Weeks, both explained with reference to "firstfruits." The "harvest" term is self-evident. The "weeks" term is not, at least until you get to Leviticus.

There, immediately following the discussion of Passover, the Israelites are instructed: "When you come into the land that I give you and reap its harvest, you shall bring the sheaf of the firstfruits of your harvest to the priest, and he shall wave the sheaf before the LORD, so that you may be accepted. On the day after the Sabbath the priest shall wave it" (Leviticus 23:10–11).

Which Sabbath exactly? That would prove to be an enormously contested question in the history of interpretation, to which we'll return in a moment. The point for now is that the very first of the firstfruits is to be offered to the Lord during or immediately after Passover. The grain in question would have been barley, which was first to ripen and did so right around the time of Passover in the land of Israel.

The instructions in Leviticus then continue, "You shall count seven full weeks from the day after the Sabbath, from the day that you brought the sheaf of the wave offering. You shall count fifty days to the day after the seventh Sabbath. Then you shall present a grain offering of new grain to the LORD" (23:15–16; cf. Numbers 28:26–31). This is where the "weeks" part comes in. In Hebrew, the word for "weeks" is Shavuot, the name still in use for this festival in Jewish observance. It has an added layer of meaning, since seven weeks could be thought of as a "week of weeks": seven days time seven weeks, for forty-nine days in all.

But Leviticus gives a second way of calculating, not by weeks but by days: "fifty days to the day after the seventh Sabbath." It's fifty days, not forty-nine, because you have the seven full weeks plus the day after, on which the festival itself takes place. Greek-speaking Jews in the ancient world named their festival according to its days rather than its weeks, with the resulting term of *pentēkostē*, meaning "fiftieth," the "day" part being implied. That, of course, is the source of the English word "Pentecost."

Back to the question of which Sabbath to count from. It could mean either the seventh day of the week, the day of rest, that fell within Passover week; or it could mean the day of Passover itself as a holy day of rest. The Torah is ambiguous, so you could go either way. Sadducees and temple priests preferred the first option.

Pharisaic Judaism, which over time became rabbinic Judaism, favored the second option, because it allowed (by a series of inferences) to link the first-ever Pentecost following *the* Passover to the exact day on which the Lord God gave the law on Mount Sinai.

A day of commemoration and celebration of the giving of the law was already desirable to those living outside the land and thus unable to make the pilgrimage to the Temple in Jerusalem; all the more so after the Temple was destroyed. Both Passover and Sukkot mandate activities you can carry on without a Temple, but all that Pentecost commands is offerings at the Temple.

So Pentecost, reinterpreted as the day of the giving of the Torah, allowed it to be observed and celebrated without a Temple and made the Torah itself the revelatory point of contact between God and his people.

Whichever Sabbath you start from, and whether you go by weeks or days, counting to reach the festival of Pentecost is of central importance. Passover and Pentecost exist in tight connection, the one linked directly to the other in time. There's a first firstfruits offering at Passover, from the barley harvest, and fifty days later a second firstfruits offering, from the "wheat harvest" (Exodus 34:22).

Notably, the offering presented at Pentecost is not raw unprocessed grain but "two loaves of bread... of fine flour, and they shall be baked with leaven, as firstfruits to the LORD" (Leviticus 23:17). The offering of leavened bread at Pentecost makes a dramatic contrast to the unleavened bread at Passover. There's no clearer sign that Passover is really and truly over.

Let's assume the Sadducees' calculation of Pentecost was in effect while the Temple was still standing. That means, counting forty-nine days from the Sabbath during Passover, and adding one more day to arrive at the festival itself, Pentecost each and every year would fall on the first day of the week, or, you might say, on the eighth day of the week.

In short, it's entirely likely that the first Christian Pentecost fell on a Sunday, the day of the week on which Jesus was raised from the dead.

Hebrew uses two words for "firstfruits": *bikkurim* and *reshith*. They are more or less interchangeable, though *bikkurim* suggests naturally occurring things and *reshith* things requiring human effort.

The feast of Pentecost doesn't even begin to exhaust the rich set of associations swirling around the notion of firstfruits in either word. In fact, there are more references to firstfruits outside the context of the festival than within it. Twice in Exodus God commands the Israelites, "The best of the firstfruits of your ground you shall bring into the house of the LORD your God" (23:19, 34:26, *bikkurim* both times). Leviticus advises on grain offerings of firstfruits (2:11–16, both *reshith* and *bikkurim*).

Numbers 15:20–21 instructs twice that "the first [*reshith*] of your dough" is to be presented as "a loaf"—which in Hebrew is *challah*! Later it also requires the first of your oil, wine, grain, and fruit (18:12–13, using both terms; cf. Deuteronomy 18:4, using *reshith*, which adds the "first fleece of your sheep," and II Chronicles 31:5, also *reshith*).

The discussion of firstfruits in Numbers leads immediately into a discussion of the firstborn, *bekor*. The obvious etymological relationship between *bikkurim* and *bekor* points up the conceptual overlap. "Everything that opens the womb of all flesh, whether man or beast, which they offer to the LORD, shall be yours. Nevertheless, the firstborn of man you shall redeem, and the firstborn of unclean animals you shall redeem... But the firstborn of a cow, or the firstborn of a sheep, or the firstborn of a goat, you shall not redeem; they are holy. You shall sprinkle their blood on the altar and shall burn their fat as a food offering, with a pleasing aroma to the LORD" (18:15, 17). As in the relationship of timing between Passover and Pentecost, so also with their offerings: you can't get too far away from sacrificial blood, even when talking about the firstfruits of grain.

Deuteronomy discusses firstfruits in anticipation of arrival in the promised land.[29] When you "have taken possession of it and live in it, you shall take some of the first of all the fruit of the ground, which you harvest from your land that the LORD your God is giving you, and you shall put it in a basket, and you shall go to the place that the LORD your God will choose, to make his name to dwell there" (26:1–2, *reshith*). In a kind of personal renewal of the covenant, you hand the basket over to the priest and say, "I declare today to the LORD your God that I have come into the land that the LORD swore to our fathers to give us" (26:3).

After the priest sets your basket of firstfruits before the altar, you recite what is effectively an Israelite creed: "A wandering Aramean was my father..." The creed recounts the sojourn in Egypt, the humiliation and toil of slavery in Egypt, the rescue by the Lord "with signs and wonders" (cf. Acts 2:22), and the gift of "this land, a land flowing with milk and honey. And behold, now I bring the first of the fruit of the ground, which you, O LORD, have given me" (Deuteronomy 26:5–10, *reshith*). Without naming the Feast of Weeks by name, the ritual action and the creed point to the same relationship of deliverance at Passover to worshipful presentation of firstfruits at Pentecost.

Just as the returned exiles resumed the practice of Sukkot in rebuilt Jerusalem, so too did they recommit themselves to offering firstfruits and firstborns. "We obligate ourselves to bring the firstfruits [*bikkurim*] of our ground and the firstfruits [*bikkurim*] of all fruit of every tree, year by year, to the house of the LORD; also to bring to the house of our God, to the priests who minister in the house of our God, the firstborn [*bekor*] of our sons and of our cattle, as it is written in the Law, and the firstborn [*bekor*] of our herds and of our flocks; and to bring the first [*reshith*] of our dough, and our contributions, the fruit of every tree, the wine and the oil, to the priests, to the chambers of the house of our God" (Nehemiah 10:35–37; cf. 12:44, 13:31; Proverbs 3:9; Ezekiel 44:30).

Firstborn and firstfruits are key concepts in apostolic teaching.

Jesus is Mary's firstborn son, presented and redeemed at the Temple. "And when the time came for their purification according to the Law of Moses, they brought him up to Jerusalem to present him to the Lord (as it is written in the Law of the Lord, 'Every male who first opens the womb shall be called holy to the Lord') and to offer a sacrifice according to what is said in the Law of the Lord, 'a pair of turtledoves, or two young pigeons'" (Luke 2:22–24).

It's an easy leap from his birth to his Resurrection. Revelation's opening image is of "Jesus Christ the faithful witness, the firstborn of the dead, and the ruler of kings on earth" (1:5). Colossians opens similarly: "He is the image of the invisible God, the firstborn of all creation... He is the beginning, the firstborn from the dead, that in everything he might be preeminent" (1:15, 18).

The firstborn logically connects to firstfruits for Paul. "Those whom [God] foreknew he also predestined to be conformed to the image of his Son, in order that he might be the firstborn among many brothers" (Romans 8:29). His brothers are believers who have received the Spirit and become co-heirs with Christ. Though not yet fully manifest as what we truly are, nevertheless we enjoy and possess "the firstfruits [*aparchēn*] of the Spirit,"[30] even as we groan inwardly awaiting our "adoption as sons, the redemption of our bodies" (8:23).

In this way and on this basis Paul regularly extends the firstfruits metaphor to believers. "But we ought always to give thanks to God for you, brothers beloved by the Lord, because God chose you as the firstfruits to be saved, through sanctification by the Spirit and belief in the truth" (II Thessalonians 2:13; cf. James 1:18 and Revelation 14:4, also calling believers *aparchḗ*). Translations obscure the same figure elsewhere: Paul speaks of the household of Stephanas as the "first-fruits [*aparchḕ*] of Achaia" (I Corinthians 16:15) and Epaenetus as the "firstfruits [*aparchḕ*] of Asia in Christ" (Romans 16:5).[31]

Paul was certainly aware of the allusion to Pentecost in firstfruits language and used it to his advantage. In his long defense of the on-going election of Israel, he rebukes Gentile pride, reminding the nations that their holiness is derivative of Israel's. "If the dough offered as firstfruits is holy," he argues, "so is the whole lump" (Romans 11:16). Not only is the word for "firstfruits" the standard Greek term in use, *aparchḗ*, but the word for "dough," *phúrama*, is the same used by the Septuagint in Numbers 15 to translate *challah*! The allusion to the festival offering at Pentecost is plain as can be. And Paul on his own account still observed Pentecost after his encounter with the risen Jesus (I Corinthians 16:8; cf. Acts 20:16).

What we have here is layered firsts. Jesus Christ is the firstborn of the dead, the firstborn of the resurrection, the first harvest in what will be a large harvest completed only at the eschaton when he comes back to gather it all up. Believers are the firstborn of the Spirit, not yet raised from the dead themselves, but by the Spirit promised to receive that gift in due course.

Paul spells it out in his discourse to the Corinthian church. "But each in his own order: Christ the firstfruits [*aparchḕ*], then at his coming [*parousía*] those who belong to Christ. Then comes the end, when he delivers the kingdom to God the Father after destroying every rule and every authority and power. For he must reign until he has put all his enemies under his feet. The last enemy to be destroyed is death" (I Corinthians 15:23–26).

What this means for us is that the time we live in is Pentecost time. All the time that is *left* is Pentecost time. When Pentecost ends, time ends, too. History ends, and Sukkot begins: the completed harvest and the merrymaking that ensues in the everlasting kingdom of God.

So back to Peter, the exemplary disciple, so right and so wrong at the same time. He was *right* to perceive in the transfigured Jesus the eschatological joy of the completed harvest. He was only *wrong* to think that the vision he beheld was the arrival of that reality. The transfigured Jesus is the sign and revelation of the goal, but not yet its completion.

How fitting, then, that the disciple who tried to hang on to the Sukkot Jesus became an unwilling eyewitness to the Passover Jesus—but who then, after his forgiveness and restoration, became the appointed preacher of the Pentecost Jesus on the Sunday of the Pentecost Spirit.

Once we see it, it couldn't be clearer. The earliest apostles and believers interpreted their experience of Jesus by way of the Scriptures, ransacking every corner to make sense of this most unusual Messiah.

In like fashion, they interpreted the Jesus they worshiped by way of worship, not least of all by the pilgrimage festivals that brought them to worship the Presence residing in the Temple at the heart of Jerusalem, the city where Jesus was crucified and raised from the dead.

If we map Jesus onto the festivals, or the festivals onto Jesus, and both onto the timeline of events, what we see is this.

The crucified Jesus is the Passover Jesus, the lamb who was slain to let the firstborn go free.

The risen Jesus is the Pentecost Jesus, the firstfruits of the resurrection who sends his Spirit on Pentecost to gather up the firstfruits of the church.

And the ascended, exalted, glorified Jesus, the one who will come again to gather up the final harvest, is the Sukkot Jesus.

Why then the Transfiguration? Isn't the Jesus revealed there out of order and way too soon?

Yes. But with a purpose.

The crucified Passover Jesus was known, seen, and even touched. Likewise, the risen Pentecost Jesus was known, seen, and even touched. But the glorified Jesus has yet to return, even now. His return, his parousia, is delayed. That made some doubt whether he really was the recipient of God's glory and honor. Some doubted whether he would come again at all. How could we ever know for sure? If we don't perdure to the end, we cannot be eyewitnesses of his return as the exalted one.

That is why the Transfiguration has to erupt in the middle of the earthly Jesus' ministry; why we get an out-of-sequence foretaste of the final Sukkot before Passover even gets underway, to say nothing of Pentecost.

The Transfiguration shows us, not his cursed destiny as the dead man on the cross, nor his vindicated destiny as the firstborn from the dead, but his eschatological destiny as Lord to whom "was given dominion and glory and a kingdom, that all peoples, nations, and languages should serve him; his dominion is an everlasting dominion, which shall not pass away, and his kingdom one that shall not be destroyed" (Daniel 7:14). Lordship belongs to "Jesus alone" (Mark 9:8).

That, finally, is why Second Peter appeals to the Transfiguration, rather than the Resurrection or any other event in the life of Christ, to make the case for the *return* of the glorified one. "For not having imitated sophisticated myths, we made known to you all the power and parousia of our Lord Jesus Christ, rather having come to be eyewitnesses of that splendor" (1:16). It is the transfigured Jesus, not the risen Jesus, who offers a glimpse of the exalted Jesus who will reign at the end of all things.

The transfigured Jesus is thus the counterargument to the scoffers who say, "Where is the promise of his coming [*parousías*]? For ever since the fathers fell asleep, all things are continuing as they were from the beginning of creation" (3:4). The Second Epistle of Peter's chief purpose is to defend the second coming of Christ, delayed as it may be. It is in this Epistle that we get the assurance that delay is divine mercy, not failure or forgetfulness: "The Lord is not slow to fulfill his promise as some count slowness, but is patient toward you, not wishing that any should perish, but that all should reach repentance" (3:9).

Second Peter is by no means the only writing of the New Testament to be concerned with the second coming of Christ—or to treat it as a separate item of concern from the Resurrection. "Parousia" quickly became a technical term, as it were, for the promised return of Jesus, contingent on and consequent to the Resurrection, but not identical with it. In Matthew's retelling of the little apocalypse of Mark 13, the word appears four times on Jesus' lips (24:3, 27, 37, 39). "Parousia" is all over the Thessalonian correspondence, which as far as we know are Paul's earliest letters and very much preoccupied with the return of Christ (I Thessalonians 2:19, 3:13, 4:15, 5:23; II Thessalonians 2:1, 8). James refers to the parousia twice (5:7, 8) and the first Johannine Epistle once (I John 2:28).

It is one thing to argue that Jesus rose from the dead. It is another to argue that the risen Jesus ascended into heaven, was exalted to his Father's right hand, and will return in glory to judge the living and the dead. Both are crucial, but each needs its own line of defense.

Now that we see the distinction between the Pentecost Jesus and the Sukkot Jesus, we can understand why the disciples did *not* understand Jesus' prophecy of the Resurrection, "disputing what it is, to rise from the dead" (Mark 9:10), any more than they understood why the Christ should have to suffer and be killed. On the mountaintop they got a glimpse not of the risen Christ but of the glorified Christ, whom they accordingly presumed to transcend space, time, and bodiliness.

It turns out the disciples had as much trouble with bodily resurrection as with bodily death. It is and remains a stumbling block, how this mortal body should put on immortality, how this site of sin and suffering should be clothed in everlasting life. A risen body on earth is a scandal in a way that an ascended body in heaven is not.

Keeping the risen Pentecost Jesus at arm's length, so to speak, from the exalted Sukkot Jesus shelters the former. The bodily risen Jesus is framed between his transfigured self, mid-stream of his career, and his glorified self, well after his Ascension, so that we can become eyewitnesses of his very fleshly victory over death. The Resurrection can't be compromised. We must confess that Jesus is victorious Lord of all—but not at the cost of losing his Resurrection. We will not be permitted any gnostic or platonic distance from the very *stuff* of the risen body of Jesus.

Matthew and Luke flesh out Mark's distinction but not separation of the risen Jesus from the transfigured and glorified Jesus by way of the Ascension. If there is a real body, raised from the dead, then you have to account for its exit from the scene. A gradually receding Jesus would be highly suspect. You'd wonder if the so-called Resurrection was real, or just a sophisticated myth. A risen Jesus *has to be*, ultimately, an ascended Jesus, too.

So in the very last verses of Matthew we behold Jesus meeting his disciples on—a mountain! Once again, it is an unspecified mountain, only "the mountain to which Jesus had directed them" (28:16). Astonishingly, while most worship him, "some doubted" (28:17). The Resurrection so confounds expectations that even being an eyewitness cannot cure spiritual blindness. Jesus has the last word in this Gospel, giving a commission to make disciples, teach, and baptize in the name of the Father and of the Son and of the Holy Spirit—framed on either side by eschatological claims: "All authority in heaven and earth has been given to me... Behold, I am with you always, to the end of the age" (28:18, 20).

Luke crafts a doublet of the Ascension, one to end his Gospel and the other to open Acts. The former account is exceedingly modest: "While he blessed them, he parted from them and was carried up into heaven" (Luke 24:51).

The latter is more detailed. At Jesus' last meeting with his disciples, they ask him if he is going to restore the kingdom now—misunderstanding both Pentecost Jesus and Sukkot Jesus in one. He advises them to give up any interest in "times or seasons that the Father has fixed by his own authority" (Acts 1:7). For there is work to do: the Pentecost Jesus will shortly hand the sickle over to the Pentecost Spirit, who will "come upon you" (1:8). Then the disciples will become his witnesses, gathering in a harvest from the very ends of the earth.

"And when he had said these things, as they were looking on, he was lifted up, and a cloud took him out of their sight" (1:9)—a cloud! "And while they were gazing into heaven as he went, behold, two men stood by them in white robes"—two otherworldly companions, and in white clothing no less! The two men advise the disciples to turn their gaze from heaven back to earth, for "this Jesus, who was taken up from you into heaven, will come in the same way as you saw him go into heaven" (1:11), just as Daniel prophesied.

It would be easy, too easy, to lose the historical, embodied Jesus in the enthralling glory of the ascended, exalted Jesus. By having the ordinary, earthly Jesus change, transform, metamorphose—*and then return to normal*—we are shown beyond any question of a doubt that it is the same Jesus all the way through: the one who was conceived by the Spirit and the one who sent the Spirit, the one who was crucified and the one who was raised, the one who walked and talked and ate and slept and the one who was taken up into heaven to be crowned, eventually to return and claim his kingdom.

The transfigured Jesus connects the historical, earthly, ordinary Jesus to the ascended, exalted, enthroned Jesus. These two are linked by their passage through the cross and Resurrection. But even with this common node between them, they are kept distinct from the risen Jesus. The bodiliness of the risen Jesus must not be undermined in any way, must not be subject to doubt, must not be transcendently whisked away with draperies of glory or lightning.

What then is the metamorphosis at the heart of the Transfiguration? For a few moments, Jesus still in his ordinary human vesture is changed into the reigning, ruling Lord of all, highly exalted, bearing the name that is above every name, at which every knee does in fact bow in heaven and on earth and under the earth. And then he changes back to ordinary humanity. For he must first make his way through Passover as the lamb and Pentecost as the firstfruits before he can return in his final role as exalted Lord of the harvest.

Will he return? We don't know. We are still in Pentecost time. The harvest is still being gathered.

In the meanwhile, the Transfiguration stands as the promise that Sukkot Jesus is coming. It is God's kindness and consolation to give us a glimpse into his Son's final victory, now, before the end, for living in these in-between times.

There is one last reason for the Transfiguration.

The Resurrection will be shared with us. Jesus Christ is the first-born of the dead, the firstfruits of the Resurrection—the first, not the last or the only. "For the trumpet will sound, and the dead will be raised imperishable, and we shall be changed" (I Corinthians 15:52).

But the Transfiguration of Jesus is not shared. It belongs to "Jesus alone" (Mark 9:8). The Transfiguration reveals what distinguishes the firstborn of the dead from all others raised from the dead: that Jesus alone is the Son of God, as much God as God is God, not only the object of God's action but the subject that is God, too. He is Lord, and we are not.

Even in our risen, imperishable bodies, we will offer our worship and praise to him. Equality with Christ is not something to grasp at. His generosity in sharing his Resurrection with us is more than enough.

Jesus' Transfiguration is *for* us. But it is not *about* us.

And now we know why the Father does not speak in the final act of Jesus' drama.

The Father speaks to his Son at the Baptism to launch him on his pilgrimage through Passover, Pentecost, and Sukkot. The Father speaks again at the Transfiguration to assure both Israel-of-old and church-soon-to-be that this talk of cross and suffering is right and good, the first step toward a cosmic Passover that will lead to the eschatological Sukkot.

But once Passover begins, once the lamb is in Jerusalem and ready to be slain, the Father no longer needs to speak. His Son speaks for him. And once Pentecost begins, once his Holy Spirit falls upon the firstfruits of believers, the Father no longer needs to speak. His Spirit speaks for him.

The Father does not need to speak, because his risen Son and his poured-out Spirit speak for him.

Will the Father ever speak again?

Maybe, at the end, when "the Son himself will also be subjected to him who put all things in subjection under him, that God may be all in all" (I Corinthians 15:28).

We will find out when the final Sukkot comes.

Afterwards

It is time to come down off the mountain.

Maybe it's a disappointment. Maybe it's sheer relief.

Things can't be the same after this, even though we are back in the company of Jesus alone, and an ordinary Jesus, at that. We can no longer evade knowledge of his cross. We cannot but wrestle with all the peculiarities of his Resurrection. We must learn to hope for his return—hard enough for the disciples back then, harder for us now, even if we strive to count the Lord's slowness as patience.

Meanwhile, there is still an enormous harvest to be gathered in. It is plentiful, but the laborers are few. We have more than enough to keep us busy as we learn to be patient with the Lord's patience.

And anyway, the ascended Lord does not leave us as orphans. He has promised to be with us until the end of the age. He has sent his Spirit to be with us forever. Present if not seen, ubiquitous yet hidden, near and aloof at once, he is not an absent Christ but a present one.

Sometimes the old hymns say in four lines what a theologian needs a whole book to express.

> How good, Lord, to be here!
> Yet we may not remain;
> But since you bid us leave the mount,
> Come with us to the plain.[32]

NOTES

PREFACE

1. The details of Transfiguration's liturgical history are drawn from *Light on the Mountain: Greek Patristic and Byzantine Homilies on the Transfiguration of the Lord*, translated and edited by Brian E. Daley SJ; Frank C. Senn's *Christian Liturgy*; Luther D. Reed's *The Lutheran Liturgy*; and Philip H. Pfatteicher's *Commentary on the Lutheran Book of Worship*.

METAMORPHOSIS

2. I infer this is why Gabriel's visit to Mary is so carefully crafted: on the one hand, to stress the redemptive initiative of the Most High in sending a Savior apart from human willpower or action; on the other hand, to distance the means by which the babe comes to be as far as possible from the endless stream of rapes perpetrated by Olympian gods on vulnerable human women. Plow through all of Ovid's *Metamorphoses* and you'll see what I mean.

3. Luke and Acts, individually and combined, far outstrip all other New Testament books for the number of references to prayer.

4. Note that in Luke's telling of Jesus' Baptism, it happens while Jesus is praying. Also, Luke interrupts the Baptism story to report John's arrest and imprisonment, and never specifies who it is that baptizes Jesus.

5. If you are puzzled and distressed that the first instance of the word in this sentence doesn't have a long mark over the o but the second one does, fear not, it's no typo. The first instance is a verb in the past tense, which takes an omicron (the "short o" in Greek), while the second is a participle and takes an omega (the "long o" in Greek).

ESCHATON

6. One of the most consistent questions I've gotten from people who've heard about this book in the making has been: how did the disciples *know* it was Moses and Elijah? Did the two men introduce

themselves? wear nametags? carry the lost tablets of the law and the reins to horses of fire? I regret to confess that this is the one question I cannot answer conclusively. But I think it's safe to assume that Jesus would know to whom he spoke.

7. Quoted from Pantoleon, "Sermon on the Most Glorious Transfiguration of Our Lord and God, Jesus Christ," in *Light on the Mountain*.

8. If you want to track the plot of John's baptism versus baptism in Jesus' name in Luke-Acts, see my book *To Baptize or Not to Baptize: A Practical Guide for Clergy*.

9. I presume this is why Luke drops the explicit association of John with Elijah in his version of Matthew 11. He's already made the point in his opening chapter, so there's no need to repeat it here.

10. Quoted from John Chrysostom, "Homily 56 on the Gospel of Matthew," in *Light on the Mountain*.

EXODUS

11. The 2021 revision of the NRSV, called the NRSVUE ("updated edition"), apparently has repented of its mealy-mouthedness, such that 9:31 now reads, "They appeared in glory and were speaking about his exodus, which he was about to fulfill in Jerusalem."

12. The NRSVUE does better than the ESV in this verse, so I have quoted it here.

13. My translation of II Corinthians 3:18.

TABERNACLES

14. Most often the biblical stories of female death are due to the bad behavior of human males, not of God. Judges is the prime example, from Jephthah's rash vow that costs his very own daughter her life to the horrifying gang rape of the Levite's concubine. Newborn, firstborn human girls do *not* have to be bought back from the Lord to spare their lives. The only time the Lord requires the life of a female is in the very few cases of female sacrificial animals (Leviticus 4:28, 4:32, 5:6, 14:10; Numbers 6:14, 15:27, 19:2–10; Deuteronomy 21:3–4). The vast majority of sacrificial animals are male, which reflects the reality of herding cultures: females are precious, preserved and

guarded to bring forth more life, whereas males are expendable and trouble to boot. The ones allowed to live are mostly castrated.

15. Quoted from Josephus, *Antiquities of the Jews* VIII.4.1.

16. The allusion to Sukkot in I Kings 8:2 is not immediately obvious. The text reads, "at the festival in the month Ethanim, which is the seventh month." The festival of the seventh month *is* Sukkot.

17. Quoted from John of Damascus, "Oration on the Transfiguration of Our Lord and Savior Jesus Christ," in *Light on the Mountain*.

18. Most Bible translations accurately if unilluminatingly call it the "Feast of Dedication" (John 10:22), which is what the word means in both Hebrew and Greek. But most readers won't realize that means Hanukkah. The events that gave rise to Hanukkah postdated the last book of the Old Testament. Which means the festival of Hanukkah is mentioned here, in the New Testament, but not at all in the Old!

19. My translation of John 1:14.

20. My translation of Revelation 21:3.

EYEWITNESSES

21. My translation of II Peter 1:13–14.

22. If I seem to be hedging my bets more than usual here, it's because that's as far as the scholarship can take me. Second Peter remains understudied and rather mysterious in its origins, and I don't feel I can make a clearer judgment call as to its origin. But I stand by its canonicity, which is the more important criterion, as far as I'm concerned.

23. Be careful sorting through Jameses and Johns. James the brother of the Lord emerges prominently in Acts, and is also mentioned by name in some of the Epistles, but he is not the son of Zebedee. There is, of course, John the Baptist, but we also have a "John whose other name was Mark" (Acts 12:12). The John who accompanies Barnabas and Saul/Paul in Acts 13 is not specified, but presumably it's John Mark, not John son of Zebedee. The only other possible appearance of the Transfiguration trio together is in Galatians 2:9, where Paul writes, "When James and Cephas [Peter] and John, who seemed to be pillars, perceived the grace that was given to me, they gave the right hand of fellowship to Barnabas and me." But from context it is

almost certain that the James in question is once again the brother of the Lord, not the brother of John son of Zebedee. This passage does, however, shore up the ongoing partnership of Peter and John son of Zebedee in their apostolic ministry.

Cloud

24. David's song invoking storm imagery continues to unfold in such a way as to make it ripe for christological harvest. "The Lord dealt with me according to my righteousness; according to the cleanness of my hands he rewarded me. For I have kept the ways of the Lord and have not wickedly departed from my God. For all his rules were before me, and from his statutes I did not turn aside. I was blameless before him, and I kept myself from guilt. And the Lord has rewarded me according to my righteousness, according to my cleanness in his sight" (22:21–25). The song concludes, "Great salvation he brings to his king, and shows steadfast love to his anointed, to David and his offspring forever" (22:51). The chief difference between David and the Son of David was that the former was rescued from his enemies, while the latter was delivered right into their hands. That forms the crux of the controversy that split the people of Israel.

25. My translation from the Greek. Please note: the Septuagint versification is different from current standard usage, so in the LXX this is Exodus 40:28–29. Any English translation you pull off the shelf (which will have been translated from Hebrew, not Greek) has it as Exodus 40:34–35.

26. The "overshadow" term also makes an appearance in Acts, and a funny one at that. "And more than ever believers were added to the Lord, multitudes of both men and women, so that they even carried out the sick into the streets and laid them on cots and mats, that as Peter came by at least his shadow might fall [*episkiásē*] on some of them" (5:14–15). No power is attributed to Peter's shadow, even by extension from his presence at the Transfiguration cloud's overshadowing, so this seems to be more a case of Luke reporting an upswelling of popular piety than making a theological assertion of his own.

PAROUSIA

27. The different ending of the Greek word for "beloved" in Mark 9 versus the Septuagint's Genesis 22 is because the former is in the nominative case, while the latter is in the accusative case.

28. It is better to read the verb here (*egerthē*) as a passive than as a deponent, hence "he has been raised" rather than "he has risen." Also, with this assertion I am agreeing with the widely held judgment that the original ending of Mark falls at 16:8.

29. While it's interesting in itself, I'll pass over this particular bit of firstfruits case law, which seems to derive directly from the crisis among Jacob's sons by different wives: "If a man has two wives, the one loved and the other unloved, and both the loved and the unloved have borne him children, and if the firstborn son belongs to the unloved, then on the day when he assigns his possessions as an inheritance to his sons, he may not treat the son of the loved as the firstborn in preference to the son of the unloved, who is the firstborn, but he shall acknowledge the firstborn, the son of the unloved, by giving him a double portion of all that he has, for he is the firstfruits of his strength. The right of the firstborn is his" (Deuteronomy 21:15–17). Firstborn sons as "firstfruits" appear in an even less appealing context when recalling the death of the Egyptian firstborn in Psalm 78:51 and 105:36.

30. The Septuagint translates *reshith* as *aparchē* (literally, "from the beginning") and *bikkurim* as *prōtogennēmata* ("first offspring"). Only *aparchē* appears in the New Testament, but it seems logically to imply both types of firstfruits.

31. My translation of I Corinthians 16:15 and Romans 16:5. The term "firstfruits" is usually translated into English as "first converts."

AFTERWARDS

32. Joseph Armitage Robinson, "How Good, Lord, To Be Here!"

BIBLIOGRAPHY

Except for the stand-alone translations between the chapters and unless otherwise indicated, all Scripture quotations are from The Holy Bible, English Standard Version, copyright © 2001 by Crossway, a publishing ministry of Good News Publishers. Used by permission. All rights reserved.

W. F. Albright and C. S. Mann, *Matthew*, The Anchor Bible vol. 26 (Garden City: Doubleday, 1971).

Andreas Andreopoulos, *This Is My Beloved Son: The Transfiguration of Christ* (Brewster: Paraclete Press, 2012).

Herbert W. Basser, "The Jewish Roots of the Transfiguration," *Bible Review* 14/3 (June 1998): 30–35.

Richard Bauckham, *Jude and 2 Peter*, Word Biblical Commentary vol. 50 (Waco: Word, 1983).

Book of Common Prayer (New York: James Pott & Co, 1892).

Kathryn Chew, "Eyeing Epiphanies in Greek, Latin, and Sanskrit Texts," *Phoenix* 65/3–4 (2011): 207–237.

B. D. Chilton, "The Transfiguration: Dominical Assurance and Apostolic Vision," *New Testament Studies* 27/1 (1980): 115–124.

A Collection of Private Devotions: in the Practice of the Ancient Church, called the Hours of Prayer... 11th ed. (London: J. G. & F. Rivington, 1838).

Jamie Davies, "Apocalyptic Topography in Mark's Gospel: Theophany and Divine Invisibility at Sinai, Horeb, and the Mount of Transfiguration," *Journal of Theological Interpretation* 14/1 (2020): 140–148.

John R. Donahue SJ and Daniel J. Harrington SJ, *The Gospel of Mark*, Sacra Pagina vol. 2 (Collegeville: Liturgical Press, 2005).

Craig A. Evans, *Mark 8:27–16:20*, Word Biblical Commentary vol. 34B (Nashville: Thomas Nelson, 2001).

Joseph A. Fitzmyer SJ, *The Gospel according to Luke (I–IX)*, The Anchor Bible vol. 28 (Garden City: Doubleday, 1981).

— , *Romans*, The Anchor Bible vol. 33 (New York: Doubleday, 1993).

Victor Paul Furnish, *II Corinthians*, The Anchor Bible vol. 32A (Garden City: Doubleday, 1984).

Lev Gillet, "Méditation sur la Fête avec le Père Lev Gillet," in *L'An de Grâce du Seigneur* (Paris: Cerf, 1988).

Donald A. Hagner, *Matthew 14–28*, Word Biblical Commentary vol. 33B (Dallas: Work Books, 2015).

Daniel J. Harrington SJ, *The Gospel of Matthew*, Sacra Pagina vol. 1 (Collegeville: Liturgical Press, 2007).

Luke Timothy Johnson, *The Gospel of Luke*, Sacra Pagina vol. 3 (Collegeville: Liturgical Press, 1991).

Josephus, *The Genuine Works of Flavius Josephus the Jewish Historian*, trans. William Whiston (London: 1737).

W. L. Liefeld, "Tranfigure," in *The New International Dictionary of New Testament Theology*, ed. Colin Brown (Grand Rapids: Zondervan, 1975).

Light on the Mountain: Greek Patristic and Byzantine Homilies on the Transfiguration of the Lord, trans. Brian E. Daley SJ, Popular Patristic Series vol. 48 (Yonkers: St. Vladimir's Seminary Press, 2013).

M. David Litwa, *Iesus Deus: The Early Christian Depiction of Jesus as a Mediterranean God* (Minneapolis: Fortress, 2014).

The Lutheran Hymnary (Minneapolis: Augsburg Publishing House, 1913).

Joel Marcus, *Mark 8–16*, The Anchor Bible vol. 27A (New Haven: Yale University Press, 2009).

Thomas W. Martin, "What Makes Glory Glorious? Reading Luke's Account of the Transfiguration Over Against Triumphalism," *Journal for the Study of the New Testament* 29/1 (2006): 3–26.

Robert J. Miller, "Is There Independent Attestation for the Transfiguration in 2 Peter?" *New Testament Studies* 42/4 (1996): 620–625.

Margaret M. Mitchell, "Epiphanic Evolutions in Earliest Christianity," *Illinois Classical Studies* 29 (2004): 183–204.

Candida R. Moss, "The Transfiguration: An Exercise in Markan Accommodation," *Biblical Interpretation* 12/1 (2004): 69–89.

Jerome H. Neyrey, *2 Peter, Jude*, The Anchor Bible vol. 37C (New York: Doubleday, 1993).

Ovid, *Metamorphoses: A New Verse Translation*, trans. David Raeburn (London: Penguin Books, 2004).

Philip H. Pfatteicher, *Commentary on the Lutheran Book of Worship* (Minneapolis: Augsburg Fortress, 1990).

John C. Poirier, "Jewish and Christian Tradition in the Transfiguration," *Revue Biblique* 111/4 (2004): 516–530.

Arthur Michael Ramsey, *The Glory of God and the Transfiguration of Christ* (London: Longmans, Green and Co., 1949).

Luther D. Reed, *The Lutheran Liturgy: A Study of the Common Liturgy of the Lutheran Church in America* (Fortress: Philadelphia, 1960).

George Robinson, *Essential Judaism: A Complete Guide to Beliefs, Customs, and Rituals* (New York: Pocket Books, 2000).

J. A. T. Robinson, "Elijah, John and Jesus: An Essay in Detection," *New Testament Studies* 4/4 (1958): 263–281.

Frank C. Senn, *Christian Liturgy: Catholic and Evangelical* (Minneapolis: Fortress, 1997).

Robert H. Stein, "Is the Transfiguration (Mark 9:2–8) a Misplaced Resurrection-Account?" *Journal of Biblical Literature* 95/1 (1976): 79–96.

Arthur Waskow, *Seasons of Our Joy: A Modern Guide to the Jewish Holidays* (Boston: Beacon Press, 1982).

Sarah Hinlicky Wilson, *To Baptize or Not to Baptize: A Practical Guide for Clergy* (St. Paul: Thornbush Press, 2021).

— , "The Verbs of the Resurrection," *Lutheran Forum* 51/2 (2017): 2–8.

SARAH HINLICKY WILSON

is the Founder of Thornbush Press.
She co-hosts the podcast
"Queen of the Sciences:
Conversations between a Theologian
and Her Dad" with Paul R. Hinlicky.
Sign up for her quarterly e-newsletter
"Theology & a Recipe"
and learn about her other books at:

www.sarahhinlickywilson.com
and
www.thornbushpress.com

by the same author

To Baptize or Not to Baptize:
A Practical Guide for Clergy

Small Catechism: Memorizing Edition

Pearly Gates:
Parables from the Final Threshold

Sermon on the Mount:
A Poetic Paraphrase

A Guide to Pentecostal Movements for Lutherans